EDWARD ALBEE'S

SEASCAPE

A Play in Two Acts

★

DRAMATISTS
PLAY SERVICE
INC.

D1269622

SEASCAPE was presented by Richard Barr, Charles Woodward and Clinton Wilder at the Shubert Theatre, in New York City, on January 26, 1975. It was directed by the author; the scenery and lighting were by James Tilton; and the costumes were by Fred Voelpel. The cast, in order of appearance, was as follows:

NANCY .... Deborah Kerr

CHARLIE .... Barry Nelson

LESLIE .... Frank Langella

SARAH .... Maureen Anderman

Production script compiled by Charles Kindl

SEASCAPE

ACT I

*Nancy and Charlie on a sand dune. Bright sun. They are
dressed informally. There is a blanket and a picnic hamper. Lunch is done; Nancy is ʋ. ʀ. ᴄ. painting seated.
Charlie is lying on blanket ʟ.*

*The curtain rises. There is a pause and then a jet plane is
heard from ʀ. to stage ʟ. Charlie sits up. Nancy stops
painting . . . looks ʟ.*

NANCY. Such noise they make.

CHARLIE. They'll crash into the dunes one day. I don't know
what good they do.

NANCY. Still . . . oh, Charlie, it's so nice! Can't we stay here forever? Please!

CHARLIE. (*Lies down.*) Huh-unh.

NANCY. That is not why. That is merely no.

CHARLIE. Because.

NANCY. Nor is that.

CHARLIE. Because . . . because you don't really mean it.

NANCY. I do!

CHARLIE. Here?

NANCY. (*Expansive.*) Yes!

CHARLIE. Right here on the beach. Build a . . . a tent, or a
lean-to.

NANCY. (*Laughs gaily.*) No, silly, not this very spot! But *here,*
by the shore.

CHARLIE. You wouldn't like it.

NANCY. I would! I'd love it here! I'd love it right where we are,
for that matter. (*Blows on painting and then puts it in paint box.*)

CHARLIE. Not after a while you wouldn't.

NANCY. Yes, I *would.* I love the water, and I love the air, and

5

the sand and the dunes and the beach grass, and the sunshine on all of it and the white clouds way off, and the sunsets and the noise the shells make in the waves and, oh, I love every bit of it. Charlie.

CHARLIE. You wouldn't. Not after a while.

NANCY. Why wouldn't I? (*Rises and goes to Charlie on the blanket.*) I don't even mind the flies and the little . . . sandfleas, I guess they are.

CHARLIE. It gets cold.

NANCY. When?

CHARLIE. In the winter. In the fall even. In spring.

NANCY. (*Laughs.*) Well, I don't mean this one, literally . . . not all the time. I mean go from beach to beach . . . live by the water. Seaside nomads, that's what we'd be. (*Sitting* R. *of Charlie on blanket.*)

CHARLIE. (*Curiously hurt feelings.*) For Christ's sake, Nancy! (*Rolling* L.)

NANCY. I mean it! Lord above! There's nothing binding us; you *hate* the city.

CHARLIE. No.

NANCY. (*Undaunted.*) It would be so lovely. Think of all the beaches we could see.

CHARLIE. No, now . . .

NANCY. Southern California, and the Gulf, and Florida . . . and up to Maine, and what's-her-name's—Martha's—Vineyard, and all those places that the fancy people go: the Riviera and that beach in Rio de Janeiro, what is that?

CHARLIE. The Copacabana.

NANCY. Yes, and Pago Pago, and . . . Hawaii! Think, Charlie! We could go around the world and never leave the beach, just move from one hot sandstrip to another: all the birds and fish and seaside flowers, and all the wondrous people that we'd meet. Oh, say you'd like to do it, Charlie.

CHARLIE. No.

NANCY. Just *say* you'd like to.

CHARLIE. If I did you'd say I meant it; you'd hold me to it.

NANCY. (*Transparent.*) No I wouldn't. Besides, you have to be pushed into everything.

6

CHARLIE. Um-hum. But I'm not going to be pushed into . . . into *this*—this new business. (*Up on* L. *elbow*.)

NANCY. (*Private rapture*.) One great seashore after another; pounding waves and quiet coves; white sand, and red, and black, somewhere, I remember reading; palms, and pine trees, cliffs and reefs and miles of jungle, sand dunes . . .

CHARLIE. No.

NANCY. . . . and all the people! Every . . . language . . . every . . . race.

CHARLIE. Unh-unh.

NANCY. Of course, I'd never push you.

CHARLIE. You? Never!

NANCY. (*Gay,*) Well, maybe a hint here; a hint there.

CHARLIE. (*Lying back down.*) Don't even do that, hunh?

NANCY. (*Leaning* L.) That's all it takes: figure out what you'd really like—what you want without knowing it, what would secretly please you, put it in your mind, then make all the plans. *You* do it; *you* like it. (*Play with sand.*)

CHARLIE. (*Up on elbows, final.*) Nancy, I don't want to travel from beach to beach, cliff to sand dune, see the races, count the flies. Anything. I don't want to do . . . anything.

NANCY. (*Testy.*) I see. Well.

CHARLIE. I'm happy . . . doing . . . nothing.

NANCY. (*Makes to gather some of their things, gets on knees, opens hamper lid, puts wine bottle in.*) Well then, we'd best get started. Up! Let's get back!

CHARLIE. (*Lies down.*) I just . . . want . . . to . . . do . . . nothing.

NANCY. (*Gathering foil wrapped items.*) Well, you're certainly not going to do that. (*Takes pillow from under his head.*) Hurry now; let's get things together.

CHARLIE. (*Aware.*) What . . . Nancy, what on earth are you . . .

NANCY. (*Busy rolling plastic fork and knife in napkin, putting in hamper with plates.*) We are *not* going to be around forever, Charlie, and you may *not* do nothing. If you don't want to do what *I* want to do—which doesn't matter—then we will do what *you* want to do, but we will not do nothing. We will do *some-*

7

thing. (*Putting paper cups in hamper.*) So, tell me what it is you want to do, and . . .

CHARLIE. I *said.* Now give me back my pillow. (*Retrieves his pillow and puts his head on it*)

NANCY. (*Last items in hamper.*) You said, "I just want to do nothing; I'm happy doing nothing." Yes? But is that what we've . . . come all this way for? (*Some wonder and chiding.*) Had the children? Spent all this time together? (*Rises and goes* R. C.) All the sharing? For nothing? To lie back down in the crib again? The same at the end as at the beginning? Sleep? Pacifier? Milk? Incomprehensible once more? (*Pause.*) Sleep? (*Pause.*) Sleep, Charlie? Back to sleep?

CHARLIE. (*Sits up.*) Well, we've earned a little rest.

NANCY. A little rest. (*Overlapping Charlie.*) (*Nods, sort of bitterly.*) We've earned a little rest. Well, why don't we act like the old folks, why don't we sell off, and take one bag apiece and go to California, (*Goes to* R. *ridge rock and sits.*) or in the desert where they have the farms—the retirement farms, the old folks' cities? Why don't we settle in to waiting, like . . . like the camels that we saw in Egypt—groan down on all fours, sigh, and eat the grass, or whatever it is. Why don't we go and wait the judgment with our peers? (*Charlie lies down.*) Take our teeth out, throw away our corset, give in to the palsy, let our mind go dim, play *Lotto* and *Canasta* with the widows and the widowers, eat cereal . . . (*Charlie sighs heavily, exasperatedly as he sits up and rolls* L.) Yes! Sigh! Go on! But once you get there, once you *do* that, there's no returning, that purgatory *before* purgatory. No thank you, sir! I've not come this long way.

CHARLIE. (*Chuckles a little, resigned.*) What do you want to do, Nancy?

NANCY. Nor have you! Not this long way to let loose. All the wisdom—by accident, by accident, some of it—all the wisdom and the . . . unfettering. (*Rises and goes to Charlie.*) My God, Charlie: See Everything Twice!

CHARLIE. (*Settling back.*) What do you want to do?

NANCY. You are *not* going to live forever, to coin a phrase. Nor am I, I suppose, come to think of it, though it would be nice; nor do I imagine we'll have the satisfaction of doing it together (*Sits on* U. C. *rock.*)—head on with a bus, or into a mountain with a

8

jet, or buried in a snow-slide, if we ever *get* to the Alps. No. I suppose I'll do the tag without you. Selfish, aren't you—right to the end.

CHARLIE. (*Lies back on elbows with hand out to Nancy.*) What do you want to do?

NANCY. (*Wistful. Rises and takes Charlie's hand as she kneels on blanket beside him.*) If you get badly sick I'll poison myself. (*Waits for reaction, gets none.*) And you?

CHARLIE. (*Yawning.*) Yes; if you get badly sick I'll poison *my*self, too.

NANCY. Yes, but then if I *did* take poison, you'd get well again, and there I'd be, laid out, all for a false alarm. I think the only thing to do is to *do* something?

CHARLIE. (*Nice.*) What would you like to do?

NANCY. (*Far away.*) Hm?

CHARLIE. Move from one sandstrip to another? Live by the sea from now on?

NANCY. (*Great wistfulness.*) Well, we have nothing holding us, except together; chattel? Does chattel mean what I think it does? We *have* nothing we *need* have. We could do it; I would so like to.

CHARLIE. (*Smiles.*) All right.

NANCY. (*Sad little laugh.*) Now, you're humoring me; it *is* something I want, though; maybe only the principle. (*Larger laugh.*) I suspect our children would have us put away if we announced it as a plan—beachcombing, leaf huts. (*Gets on knees and closes hamper lid.*) Even if we did it in hotels they'd have a case—for our *reasons.*

CHARLIE. Mmmmmmmm.

NANCY. No, let's merely have it for today . . . and tomorrow, and . . . who knows: continue the temporary and it becomes forever.

CHARLIE. (*Relaxed; content.*) All right. (*The sound of the jet plane from R. to L.—growing, becoming deafeningly loud, diminishing. Nancy rises, going to third step U. R. Charlie sits up.*)

NANCY. Such noise they make!

CHARLIE. They'll crash into the dunes one day; I don't know what good they do.

NANCY. (*After a pause.*) Still . . . ahhh; breathe the sea air.

9

(*Tiny pause; suddenly remembers.*) Didn't you tell me? When you were a little boy you wanted to live in the sea?

CHARLIE. Under.

NANCY. (*Delighted.*) Yes! Under the water—in it. That all your friends pined to have wings? Icarus? Soar?

CHARLIE. Uh-huh.

NANCY. Yes, but you wanted to go under. Gills, too?

CHARLIE. As I remember. A regular fish, (*Nancy sits at paint box* U. R. C.) I mean fishlike—arms and legs and everything, but be able to go under, live down in the coral and the ferns, come home for lunch and bed and stories, of course, but down in the green, the purple, and big enough not to be eaten if I stayed close in. Oh yes; I *did* want that.

NANCY. (*Considers it, with some wonder.*) Be a fish. (*Lightly.*) No, that's not among what *I* wanted—when *I* was little, not that I remember. I wanted to be a pony, once, I think, but not for very long. I wanted to be a *woman.* I wanted to grow up to be *that,* and all it had with it. (*Notices something below her in the distance,* U. R. *Off-hand. Charlie lies down.*) There are some people down there; I thought we were alone; in the water; some people, I think. (*Back*) And, I suppose I *have* become that.

CHARLIE. (*Smiling.*) *You* have.

NANCY. In any event the appearances of it: husband, children—precarious, those, for a while, but nicely settled now—to all appearances—and the grandchildren . . . here, and on the way. The top of the pyramid! Us two, the children, and all of theirs. (*Mildly puzzled.*) Isn't it odd that you can build a pyramid from the top down? Isn't that difficult? The engineering?

CHARLIE. (*Sits up.*) There wasn't anyone before us?

NANCY. (*Laughs lightly.*) Well, yes, but everybody builds his own, starts fresh, starts up in the air, builds the base around him. Such levitation! Our own have started *theirs.*

CHARLIE. It's all one. (*Rises goes to* L. *rock, dusting sand off his trousers.*)

NANCY. (*Sort of sad about it.*) Yes. (*Bright again.*) Or maybe it's the most . . . difficult, the most . . . breathtaking of all: the whole thing balanced on one point; a reversed *pyramid,* always in danger of toppling over when people don't behave themselves.

CHARLIE. (*Chuckling.*) All right.

NANCY. (*Above it.*) You have no interest in imagery. None.

CHARLIE. (*Defiance; rue.*) Well, I used to.

NANCY. (*Picking up painting.*) The man who married a dumb wife; not you! Was that Moliere? Beaumarchais?

CHARLIE. Anatole France.

NANCY. Was it?

CHARLIE. (*Continuing from before.*) I used to go way down; at our summer place; a protected cove. The breakers would come in with a storm, or a high wind, but not usually. I used to go way down, and try to stay. (*Nancy resumes painting.*) I remember before that, when I was tiny, I would go in the swimming pool, at the shallow end, let out my breath and sit on the bottom; when you let out your breath—all of it—you sink, gently, and you can sit on the bottom until your lungs need air. I would do that—I was so young—sit there, gaze about. Great trouble for my parents. "Good God, go get Charlie; he's gone and sunk again." "Will you look at that child? Put him in the water and he drops like a stone. (*Nancy laughs as she puts painting in box and closes water container.*) I could swim perfectly well, as easy as walking, and around the same time, but I used to love to sink. And when I was older, we were by the sea. Twelve; yes, or thirteen. I used to lie on the warm boulders, strip off . . ". (*Quiet, sad amusement.*) . . . learn about my body; no one saw me; twelve, or thirteen. And I would go into the water, take two stones, as large as I could manage, swim out a bit, tread, look up one final time at the sky . . . relax . . . begin to go down. Oh, twenty feet, fifteen, soft landing without a sound, the white sand clouding up where your feet touch, and all around you ferns . . . (*Sits* L. *ridge rock.*) and lichen. You can stay down there so long! You can build it up, and last . . . so long, enough for the sand to settle and the fish come back. And they do—come back, all sizes, some slowly, eyeing past; some streak, and you think for a moment they're larger than they are, sharks, maybe, but they never are, and one stops being an intruder, finally—just one more object come to the bottom, or living thing, part of the undulation and the silence. It was very good.

NANCY. (*Putting water container in paint box.*) Did the fish talk to you? I mean, did they come up and stay close, and look at you, and maybe nibble at your toes?

11

CHARLIE. (*Very shy.*) Some of them.

NANCY. (*Enthusiastic.*) Why don't you go and do it! Yes!

CHARLIE. (*Age.*) Oh, no, now, Nancy, I couldn't.

NANCY. Yes! Yes, you could! Go do it again; you'd love it!

CHARLIE. Oh, no, now, Nancy.

NANCY. Go down to the edge; go in! Pick up some stones . . .

CHARLIE. (*Indicates* U. L.) There're no coves; it's all open beach.

NANCY. Oh, you'll find a cove; go on! Be young again; my God, Charlie, be young!

CHARLIE. No; besides, someone'd see me; they'd think I was drowning.

NANCY. Who's to see you!? (*Looks* R.) Look, there's no one in the . . . no, those . . . people, they've come out, the ones were in the water, they're . . . well, they're lying on the beach, to sun; they're prone. (*Rises and dusts off sand.*) Go on down; I'll watch you from here.

CHARLIE. (*Firm, through embarrassment.*) No! I said no!

NANCY. (*Undaunted; still happy, goes to Charlie.*) All right then, I'll come with you; I'll stand by the edge, and if anyone comes by and says, "Look, there's a man drowning!" I'll laugh and say, "La! It's my husband, and he's gone down with two stones to sit on the bottom for a while." (*Touches Charlie's back.*)

CHARLIE. No! (*Tries to pull away.*)

NANCY. The white sand clouding, and the ferns and the lichen. Oh, do it, Charlie!

CHARLIE. (*Rises, goes to* L. *rock.*) I wouldn't like it anymore.

NANCY. (*Crosses* L. C. *Wheedling, taunting.*) Awwww, how long since you've done it?!

CHARLIE. (*Mumbles.*) Too long.

NANCY. What?

CHARLIE. (*Embarrassed; shy.*) Not since I was seventeen?

NANCY. (*This time pretending not to hear.*) What?

CHARLIE. (*Rather savage; phlegm in the throat.*) Too long. (*Small pause.*) Far too long? (*Sits* L. *rock. A pause.*)

NANCY. (*Very gentle; not even urging.*)Would it be so very hard now. (*Goes to* L. *ridge rock and sits.*) Wouldn't you be able to? Gently? In some sheltered place, not very deep? Go down? Not long, just enough to . . . reconfirm.

CHARLIE. (*Flat.*) I'd rather remember.

NANCY. If *I* were a man—what a silly thing to say.

CHARLIE. Yes, it is.

NANCY. Still, if I were . . . I don't think I'd let the chance go by; not if I had it.

CHARLIE. (*Quietly.*) Let it go.

NANCY. Not if *I* had it. There isn't that much. Sex goes . . . diminishes; well, it becomes a holiday and rather special, and not like eating, or going to sleep. But that's nice, too—that it becomes special—(*Laughs gaily.*) Do you know, I had a week when I ːnought of divorcing you? (*Brushing sand from toes.*)

CHARLIE. (*Quite surprised, vulnerable; shakes his head.*) No.

NANCY. Yes. You were having your thing, your melancholia—poor darling—and there I was, brisk and thirty, still pert, learning the moles on your back instead of your chest hairs.

CHARLIE. (*Relieved, if sad.*) Ah. Then.

NANCY. (*Nods.*) Umh-hum. Then. Rereading Proust, if I have it right. (*Rises and crosses* D. R.) Propped up in bed, all pink and ribbons, smelling good, not all those creams and looking ten years married as I might have, and who would have blamed me, but fresh, and damned attractive, if I have to say it for myself; (*Crosses* U. R.) propped up in bed, literate, sweet-smelling, getting familiar with your back. One, two, three moles, and then a pair of them, twins, flat black ones . . .

CHARLIE. (*Recalling.*) *That* time.

NANCY. (*Nods.*) . . . ummmm. The ones I said should go—*still* think they should—not that it matters: they haven't done anything. (*Goes to* C. *rock and sits.*) It was at the . . . center of your thing, your seven-month decline; it was *then* that I thought of divorcing you. The deeper your inertia went, the more *I* felt alive. Good wife, patient, see him through it, whatever it is, wonder if it isn't something *you* haven't done, or have; write home for some advice, but oh, so busy, with the children and the house. Stay neat; don't pry; weather it. But right in the center, three-and-a-half months in, it occurred to me that there was nothing wrong, save perhaps another woman.

CHARLIE. (*Surprised; hurt.*) Oh, Nancy.

NANCY. Well, one has a mind, and it goes about its business. If one is happy, *and* content, it doesn't mean that everyone else is;

13

never assume that. Maybe he's found a girl; not even looking, necessarily; maybe he turned a corner one afternoon and there was a girl, not prettier even, maybe a little plain, but unencumbered, or lonely, or lost. That's the way it starts, as often as not. No sudden passion over champagne glasses at the fancy ball, or seeing the puppy love again, never like that except for fiction, but something . . . different, maybe even a little . . . less: the relief of that; simpler, not quite so nice, how much nicer, for a little.

CHARLIE. *Nothing* like that.

NANCY. (*Laughs a little.*) Well, *I* know.

CHARLIE. Nothing at *all*.

NANCY. Yes, but the *mind*. And what bothered me was not what *you* might be doing—oh, well, certainly; *bothered*, yes—not entirely what you might be doing, but that, all of a sudden, *I* had not. (*Rises and kneels at hamper closing lid.*) *Ever*. Had not even thought of it. A child at thirty, I suppose. Without that time I would have gone through my entire life and never thought of another man, another pair of arms, harsh cheek, hard buttocks, pleasure, never at all. (*Considers that.*) Well, I might have, and maybe this was better. (*Puts hamper* L. *of* C. *rock-pillow on top.*) All at once I thought: it was over between us—not our life together, that would go on, and we would be like a minister and his sister—the . . . (*Rises, crossing* D. R. C.) active part of our life, the rough-and-tumble in the sheets or in the grass when we took our picnics, that all of that had stopped between us, or would become cursory, and I wouldn't have asked why, nor would you have said, or if I *had*—asked why—you would have said some lie, or truth, would have made it worse, (*Sits on blanket.*) and I thought back to before I married you, and the boys I would have done it with, if I had been that type, the firm-fleshed boys I would have taken in my arms had it occurred to me. And I began to think of them, Proust running on, pink and ribbons, looking at your back, and your back would turn and it would be Johnny Smythe or the Devlin boy, or one of the others, and he would smile, reach out a hand, undo my ribbons, draw me close, ease on. Oh, that was a troubling time.

CHARLIE. (*Sad remembrance.*) You were never one for the boys, were you?

NANCY. (*She, too.*) No. (*Pause.*) But I thought: well, if he can

14

turn his back on me like this (*Rises.*)—nice, isn't it, when the real and the figurative come together—*I* can turn, too, if not my back, then . . . back. (*Crosses* D. R. C.) I can have me a divorce, I thought, become eighteen again. (*Sudden thought as she picks up something.*) You know, I think that's why our women want divorces, as often as not—to be eighteen again, no matter how old they are; and daring. To do it differently, and still for the first time. (*Sighs and goes to* R. *ridge and sits.*) But it was only a week I thought about that. It went away. You came back . . . eventually.

CHARLIE. (*A statement of fact which is really a question.*) You never thought I went to anyone else.

NANCY. She said to me—wise woman—"daughter, if it lasts, if you and he come back together, it'll be at a price or two. If it lasts there'll be accommodation, wandering; if he doesn't do it in the flesh, he'll think about it; one night, in the dark, if you listen hard enough, you'll hear him think the name of another woman, kiss *her,* touch *her* breasts as he has his hand and mouth on you. Then you'll know something about loneliness, my daughter; yessiree; you'll be halfway there, halfway to compassion."

CHARLIE. (*After a pause; shy.*) And the other half?

NANCY. Hm? (*Matter-of-fact.*) Knowing how lonely *he* is . . . substituting . . . using a person, a body, and wishing it was someone else—almost anyone. *That* void. La petite morte, the French call the moment of climax? And that lovely writer? Who talks of the sadness after love? After intimate intercourse, I think he says? But what of *during?* What of the loneliness and death *then?* *During.* They don't talk of that: the sad fantasies; the substitutions. The thoughts we have. (*Tiny pause.*) *One* has.

CHARLIE. (*Rises and crosses to Nancy. Softly, with a timid smile.*) I've never been with another woman.

NANCY. (*A little laugh.*) Well, *I* know.

CHARLIE. (*Laughs ruefully.*) I think one time, when you and I were making love—when we were nearly there, I remember I pretended it was a week or so before, one surprising time we'd had, something we'd hit upon by accident or decided to do finally; (*Crosses away.*) I pretended it was the time before, and it was quite good that way.

NANCY. (*Some wonder.*) You pretended I was me.

CHARLIE. (*Apology.*) Well . . . yes.

15

NANCY. (*Laughs delightedly; thinks.*) Well; perhaps I was. (*Pause.*) So much goes, Charlie; we shouldn't give up until we have to. (*Rises. Crosses to Charlie. Gentle.*) Why don't you go down; why don't you find a cove?

CHARLIE. (*Smiles; shakes his head.*) No.

NANCY. It's something *I've* never done; you could teach me. (*Takes Charlie's hand.*) You could take my hand; we could have two big stones, and we could go down together. (*Pulls Charlie* R.)

CHARLIE. (*Not a complaint; an evasion.*) I haven't got my suit.

NANCY. Go bare! You're quite presentable.

CHARLIE. (*Mildly put off, and a little pleased.*) Nancy! (*Goes to blanket, letting go Nancy's hand.*)

NANCY. (*Almost shy.*) I wouldn't mind. I'd like to see you, pink against the blue, (*Goes top of steps.*) watch the water on you.

CHARLIE. Tomorrow.

NANCY. Bare?

CHARLIE. We'll see. (*Lays on blanket.*)

NANCY. (*Shrugs.*) I'm used to that: we'll see, and then put off until it's forgotten. (*Peers* R.) I wonder where they've gone.

CHARLIE. (*Not interested.*) Who? (*Up on right elbow.*)

NANCY. Those people; well, those that were down there.

CHARLIE. Gone in.

NANCY. What? The water? Again?

CHARLIE. No. Home.

NANCY. Well, I don't think so. I thought maybe they were coming up to us.

CHARLIE. Why?

NANCY. They . . . looked to be. I mean, I thought (*Sits at paint box.*) . . . well, no matter.

CHARLIE. Who were they?

NANCY. You know my eyes. I thought they were climbing, coming up to see us. (*Closes top of paint box.*)

CHARLIE. If we don't know them?

NANCY. *Some* people are adventurous.

CHARLIE. Mmmmm. (*Leans back on both elbows.*)

NANCY. I wonder where they've gone. (*Getting on knees, peering* R.)

CHARLIE. Don't spy!

NANCY. (*Looking down.*) I'm not; I just want to see. Lord,

16

why couldn't my ears be going instead? I think I see them half-way up the dune. I think I can make them out; resting, or maybe sunning, on an angle for the sun.

CHARLIE. A lot of good *you'd* be under water.

NANCY. (*Considers what she has seen.*) Rather odd. (*Dismisses it. Crosses to* R. *of Charlie, sitting on blanket.*) Well, that's why you'll have to take me if I'm going to go down; you wouldn't want to lose me in the fernery, and all. An eddy, or whatever that is the tide does underneath, might come along and sweep me into a cave, or culvert, and I wouldn't know *what* to do. No, you'll have to take me.

CHARLIE. You'd probably panic . . . if I took you under. (*Thinks about it.*) No; you wouldn't; you'd do worse, most likely: start drowning and not let on. (*They both laugh.*) You're a good wife. (*Pats Nancy's shoulder and lies down on blanket.*)

NANCY. (*Off-hand.*) Well, *you've* been a good husband . . . more or less. (*Lies back on elbows.*)

CHARLIE. (*Not aggressive.*) Damned right.

NANCY. *And* you courted me the way I wanted.

CHARLIE. Yes.

NANCY. *And* you gave me the children I wanted, as many, and when.

CHARLIE. Yes.

NANCY. *And* you've provided a sturdy shoulder and a comfortable life. No?

CHARLIE. *Yes.*

NANCY. And I've not a complaint in my head, have I?

CHARLIE. No.

NANCY. (*Slightly bitter.*) Well, we'll wrap you in the flag when you're gone, and do taps. (*A fair silence.*)

CHARLIE. (*Sits up. Soft; embarrassed.*) We'd better . . . gather up; . . . we should go back now.

NANCY. (*Touches him on the shoulder.*) Ohhhhhhhh . . . (*Charlie rises and steps* L. *Ibid.*) Ohhhhhhhh . . .

CHARLIE. I don't want to stay here any more. You've hurt my feelings, damn it!

NANCY. (*Sits up. Sorry.*) Ohhh, Charlie.

CHARLIE. (*Trying to understand.*) You're not cruel by nature; it's not your way. Why do you *do* this? Even so rarely; *why?*

17

NANCY. (*As if it explained everything.*) I was being *pet*ulant.

CHARLIE. (*More or less to himself, but not sotto voce.*) I *have* been a good husband to you; I *did* court you like a gentleman; I *have* been a good lover . . .

NANCY. (*Light.*) Well, of course I have no one to compare you with.

CHARLIE. (*Preoccupied; right on.*) . . . you *have* been comfortable, and my shoulder *has* been there.

NANCY. (*Gaily.*) I *know*; I *know*.

CHARLIE. You've had a good *life.*

NANCY. Don't *say* that!

CHARLIE. And you'll not pack it up in a piece of cloth and put it away.

NANCY. No! Not if *you* won't! Besides, it was hyperbole.

CHARLIE. (*Slightly testy.*) *I* knew that. Not if *I* won't, eh? Not if I won't what?

NANCY. Pack it up in a piece of cloth and put it away. When's the last time you were stung by a bee, Charlie? Was it that time in Maine . . . or Delaware? (*Gets up on knees.*) When your cheek swelled up, and you kept saying, "Mud! Get me some mud!" And there wasn't any mud that *I* could see, and you said, "Well, *make* some."

CHARLIE. Delaware. (*Goes above Nancy to* R.)

NANCY. After all the years of making you things, my mind couldn't focus on how to make *mud.* What *is* the recipe for *that,* I said to myself . . . what sort of *pan* do I use, for one; water, yes, but water and . . . what? Earth, naturally, but what *kind* and . . . oh, I felt so foolish.

CHARLIE. (*Softer.*) It was Delaware.

NANCY. *So* foolish.

CHARLIE. (*Crosses in to Nancy. Mildly reproachful.*) The whole cheek swelled up; the eye was half closed.

NANCY. (*Pedagogic.*) Well, that's what a bee sting does, Charlie. And that's what brings on the petulance—mine; it's just like a bee sting, and I remember, though it's been years.

CHARLIE. (*To reassure himself.*) Crazy as a loon. (*Turns away.*)

NANCY. No; not at all. You asked me about the petulance—why it comes on me, even rarely. Well, it's like the sting of a bee: something you say, or do; or don't say, or don't do. And it brings

18

the petulance on me, not that I like it, but it's a healthy sign, shows I'm still nicely alive.

CHARLIE. (*Turns in. Not too friendly.*) Like when? Like what?

NANCY. What brings it on, and when?

CHARLIE. (*Impatient.*) Yes!

NANCY. Well, so many things.

CHARLIE. Give me *one*.

NANCY. No; I'll give you several.

CHARLIE. (*Steps in.*) All *right*.

NANCY. "You've had a good life." (*Pause.*)

CHARLIE. (*Curiously angry.*) *All* right. Go on.

NANCY. Do you know what I'm *saying*?

CHARLIE. You're throwing it up to me; you're telling me I've had a good life.

NANCY. No-no-no! I'm saying what you *said*, what you told *me*. You told me, you said to me, "You've had a good life." I wasn't talking about *you*, though you *have*. I was saying what you said to me.

CHARLIE. (*Annoyed.*) Well, you have! You *have* had!

NANCY. (*She, too.*) Yes! Have *had*! What about that!

CHARLIE. What about it!

NANCY. *Am* not *having*. (*Waits for reaction; gets none.*) Am not *having*? Am not *having* a good life?

CHARLIE. Well, of *course*!

NANCY. Then why say had? Why put it that way?

CHARLIE. It's a way of speaking!

NANCY. No! It's a way of thinking! (*Charlie steps away.*) *I* know the language, and I know *you*. You're not careless with it, or didn't used to be. Why *not* go to those places in the desert and let our heads deflate, if it's all in the past? Why not just *do* that?

CHARLIE. (*Steps in.*) It was a way of speaking.

NANCY. Dear God, we're *here*. (*Charlie goes* D. R. C. *and sits.*) We've served our time, Charlie, and there's nothing telling us do *that*, (*Crawls to* L. *of Charlie and sits on haunches.*) or any conditional; not any more. Well, there's the arthritis in my wrist, of course, and the eyes have known a better season, and there's always the cancer or a heart attack to think about if we're bored, but beside all these things . . . what is there?

CHARLIE. (*Some triste.*) You're at it again.

19

NANCY. I am! Words are lies; they *can* be, and you *use* them, but I know what's in your gut. I *told* you, didn't I?

CHARLIE. (*Passing it off.*) Sure, sure.

NANCY. (*Mimicking.*) Sure, sure. Well, they are, and you do. What *have* we got left?

CHARLIE. (*Turns in.*) What! You mean besides the house, the kids, *their* kids, friends, all that? What?!

NANCY. Two things!

CHARLIE. Yeah?

NANCY. Ourselves and some time. (*Charlie turns away.*) Charlie; the pyramid's building by itself; the earth's spinning in its own fashion without any push from us; we've done all we ought to— and isn't it splendid we've enjoyed so much of it.

CHARLIE. (*Mild irony.*) We're pretty splendid people. (*Rises and goes to blanket.*)

NANCY. Damned right we are, and now we've got each other and some time, and all *you* want to do is become a vegetable.

CHARLIE. (*Turn back.*) Fair, as usual.

NANCY. (*Shrugs.*) All right: a lump.

CHARLIE. We've earned a little rest. (*Lying down on* L. *blanket.*)

NANCY. (*Nods.*) . . . a little rest. (*Rises.*) My God, you say that twice a day, and sometimes in-between. (*Mutters.*) We've earned a little *life,* if you ask *me.* (*Pause.*) Ask me.

CHARLIE. (*Some rue.*) No; you'd tell me. (*Sits up and rolls* L.)

NANCY. (*Bold and recriminating.*) Sure! 'Course I would! (*Sits blanket,* R. *of Charlie.*) When else are we going to get it?

CHARLIE. (*Turns in. Quite serious; quite bewildered.*) What's to be gained? And what would we really get? Some . . . illusion, I suppose; some smoke. There'd be the same sounds in the dark— or similar ones; we'd have to sleep and wonder if we'd waken, either way. It's six of one, except we'll do it on familiar ground, if *I* have *my* way. I'm not up to the glaciers and the crags, and I don't think you'd be . . . once you got out there.

NANCY. (*Grudging.*) I do admit, you make it sound scary— first time away to camp; sleeping out, the hoot owls and the goblins. Oh, that's scarey. Are you telling me you're all caved in, Charlie?

CHARLIE. (*Pause; considers the fact.*) Maybe.

NANCY. (*Pause while she ponders this.*) All closed down. Then

20

. . . what's the difference? You make it ugly enough, either way. The glaciers and the crags? At least we've never *tried that.*

CHARLIE. (*Trying to justify, but without much enthusiasm.*) There's comfort in settling in. (*Pause.*)

NANCY. Small. (*Pause.*)

CHARLIE. (*Final.*) Some. (*A silence. Leslie [a sea creature] appears, pops up, upper half of trunk, U. L. C., from behind the dune. Neither Charlie nor Nancy see him. Leslie looks at the two of them, pops back down out of sight.*)

NANCY. (*To bring them back to life again.*) Well. I've got to do some postcards tonight; tell all the folks where we are.

CHARLIE. Yes?

NANCY. . . . what a time we're having. I've got a list . . . some where. It wouldn't be nice not to. They do it for us, and it's such fun getting them.

CHARLIE. Um-hum.

NANCY. You do some, too?

CHARLIE. You do them for both of us.

NANCY. (*Mildly disappointed.*) Oh. (*Pause.*) All right.

CHARLIE. (*Not very interested.*) What do you want to do then?

NANCY. Oh, I don't know. Do you want to have your nap? Cover your face if you do, though; put something on it. *Or . . .* we could go on back. *Or . . .* we *could* do a stroll down the beach. (*While Nancy speaks, Leslie and Sarah [another sea creature] come up on the dune, behind Charlie and Nancy, but some distance away. Leslie is U. L. C. and Sarah appears U. R.*) If you won't go in, we'll find some pretty shells . . . *I* will.

CHARLIE. (*Small smile.*) What a wealth.

NANCY. (*Fairly cheerful.*) Well . . . we make the best of it. (*Charlie senses something behind him. Sits up, turns his head, sees Leslie and Sarah. His mouth falls open; he gasps. Nancy sees what Charlie is doing, is momentarily puzzled. Then she looks behind her. She sees Leslie and Sarah. Nancy, straightening her back abruptly.*) My goodness!

CHARLIE. (*Falls backwards.*) Ohmygod.

NANCY. (*Great wonder.*) Charlie!

CHARLIE. (*Eyes steady on Leslie and Sarah.*) Oh my loving God.

21

NANCY. (*Enthusiasm.*) Charlie! (*Crawls* U. *toward lizards.*)
What *are* they?!
CHARLIE. Nancy, get back here!
NANCY. But, Charlie . . .
CHARLIE. (*Deep in his throat; trying to whisper.*) Get back
here! (*Nancy crawls back until she and Charlie are together. Leslie
and Sarah look at one another, then back at Nancy and Charlie.
Charlie gets close to Nancy and whispers.*) Get a stick!
NANCY. (*Interest and wonder.*) Charlie, what are they? (*Turn-
ing to Charlie so to be in profile to audience.*)
CHARLIE. (*Urgent.*) Get me a stick!
NANCY. A what?
CHARLIE. (*Louder.*) A stick!
NANCY. (*Looking about; uncertain.*) Well . . . what *sort* of
stick, Charlie?
CHARLIE. A stick! A wooden *stick!*
NANCY. (*Turns three quarters front.*) Well, of course a wooden
stick, Charlie; what other kinds of sticks *are* there, for heaven's
sake? But, what sort of stick?
CHARLIE. (*Never taking his eyes off Leslie and Sarah.*) A big
one! A big stick!
NANCY. (*None too happy about it.*) Well . . . I'll *look.* Drift-
wood, I suppose . . . (*Crawls* D. R.)
CHARLIE. Well, of course a *wooden* stick, Charlie; what other
kinds of sticks are there? (*Leslie moves a little, maybe raises an
arm.*) GET ME A GUN!
NANCY. (*Turns back. Astonished.*) A *gun,* Charlie! Where on
earth would anyone find a gun up here? . . .
CHARLIE. (*Shrill.*) Get me a stick!
NANCY. (*Crosses.*) All right! (*Crawls* R.)
CHARLIE. Hurry!
NANCY. I'm looking! (*Crawling up* D. R. *dune.*)
CHARLIE. (*Leslie moves on top* U. L. C. *ridge. A bleak fact, to
himself as much as anything.*) They're going to come at us, Nancy
. . . (*An afterthought.*) . . . and we're arguing.
NANCY. (*Waving a smallish stick; thin, twig-like, crooked, 18
inches, maybe*) I found one, Charlie; Charlie, I found one!
CHARLIE. (*Not taking his gaze off Leslie and Sarah.*) Well,
bring it here. (*Getting on knees.*)

NANCY. (*Crawling to Charlie with the stick between her teeth.*) It's the best I could do under the circumstances. There was a big trunk or something . . .

CHARLIE. (*His arm out.*) Give it to me!

NANCY. Here! (*Gives the stick to Charlie, who, without looking at it, raises it in his right hand.*) Charlie! They're magnificent!

CHARLIE. (*Crawls to Nancy. Realizes what he is brandishing, looks at it with distaste and loss.*) What's *this?*

NANCY. It's your stick.

CHARLIE. (*Almost crying.*) Oh my God.

NANCY. (*Eyes on Leslie and Sarah.*) Charlie, I think they're absolutely beautiful. What *are* they?

CHARLIE. What am I supposed to *do* with it?!

NANCY. You asked for it, Charlie; you said you wanted it.

CHARLIE. (*Snorts; ironic-pathetic.*) Go down fighting, eh? (*Leslie clears his throat; it is a short, large sound, rather like a growl. Instinctively, Charlie and Nancy recoil.*)

NANCY. (*Not at all sure of herself.*) Fight, Charlie? Fight? Are they going to hurt us?

CHARLIE. (*Laughing at the absurdity.*) Oh God!

NANCY. Well, at least we'll be together. (*Leslie clears his throat again, same sound; Charlie and Nancy react a little, tense. Leslie picks up a large stick, four feet long and stout; he brandishes it while on his knees.*) Now, *that's* an impressive stick.

CHARLIE. (*Shakes his stick at her.*) Yeah; thanks.

NANCY. (*Some pique.*) Well, thank *you* very much. If I'd known I was supposed to go over there and crawl around under their flippers, or pads, or whatever they have . . .

CHARLIE. (*Final words; some haste.*) I love you, Nancy.

NANCY. (*The tiniest pause; a trifle begrudging.*) Well . . . I love you, too. (*Leslie slowly, so slowly, raises his stick above him in a gesture of such strength that should he smite the earth it would tremble. He holds the stick thus, rising slowly.*)

CHARLIE. Well, I certainly hope so because here they come. (*Suddenly the sound of the jet plane again, lower and louder this time, going L. to R. Leslie and Sarah react as animals would; frozen for an instant, tense, aware of danger, poised, every muscle taut, and then the two of them disappear over back of dune. Sarah pops down and Leslie jumps over back of top dune with*) *the stick. Charlie and Nancy are as if struck dumb; they stare, open-mouthed, at the now vacated dune.*)

NANCY. (*Finally, with great awe.*) Charlie! (*Infinite wonder.*) What have we *seen!?*

CHARLIE. (*Kneeling on one leg, facing front.*) The glaciers and the crags, Nancy. You'll never be closer.

NANCY. All at *once!* There they *were.* Charlie!

CHARLIE. (*Snaps fingers.*) It was the liver paste. That explains everything.

NANCY. (*Tolerant smile.*) Oh, yes; certainly.

CHARLIE. I'm sure it was the liver paste. I knew it. When you were packing the lunch this morning, I said what is that? And you said it's liver paste, for sandwiches; what's the matter? Don't you like liver paste any more? And I said, what do we need *that* for? For sandwiches, you said. And I said yes, but what do we *need* it for?

NANCY. But, Charlie . . .

CHARLIE. (*Sits.*) You've got a roasted chicken there, and peaches, and a brie, and bread and wine, what do we need the sandwiches for, the liver paste?

NANCY. You might want them, I said.

CHARLIE. But, with all the rest.

NANCY. Besides, I asked you what would happen if you picked up the roasted chicken and dropped it in the sand. What would you do; rinse it off with the wine? Then I'd have to make iced tea, too. Miles up on the dunes, no fresh water anywhere? Bring a thermos of iced tea, too, in case you dropped the chicken in the sand?

CHARLIE. *When* have I dropped a chicken in the sand? *When* have I done that?

NANCY. (*Mildly piqued.*) I wasn't suggesting it was a thing you *did;* I wasn't pointing to a history of it; I said you *might.* But, Charlie . . . at a time like *this* . . . they may come back.

CHARLIE. Liver paste doesn't keep; I *told* you that: goes bad in a minute, with the heat, and all.

NANCY. Wrapped up in silver foil.

CHARLIE. Aluminum. (*Sarah appears* U. L. C., *over dune.*)

NANCY. . . . whatever; wrapped up and perfectly safe, it keeps.

CHARLIE. It goes bad in a minute, which is what it did: the

24

liver paste clearly went bad. (*Nancy sees Sarah whereupon Sarah disappears.*) It went bad in the sun and it poisoned us.

NANCY. Pardon? (*Up on her knees.*)

CHARLIE. (*Dogmatic; glum.*) It went bad, as I said it would; the liver paste, for all your wrapping up. It went bad, and it poisoned us; *that's* what happened!

NANCY. *Poisoned* us!? (*Disbelieving, and distracted.*) And *then* what happened?

CHARLIE. (*Looks at her as if she's simpleminded.*) Why . . . we *died*, of course.

NANCY. We died?

CHARLIE. We ate the liver paste and we died. (*Leslie appears* u. l. c. *followed by Sarah. Nancy sinks on haunches as she sees the lizards.*) That drowsy feeling—the sun—and the wine—none of it: all those night thoughts of what it would be like, the sudden scalding in the center of the chest, or wasting away, milk in the eyes, voices from the other room; none of it. Chew your warm sandwich, wash it down, lie back and let the poison have its way . . . (*Leslie crawls over Sarah, getting* r. *of Sarah on top dune. Nancy begins laughing.*) . . . talk—think you're talking—and all the while the cells are curling up, disconnecting . . . Nancy, don't do that! Don't laugh at me! . . . it all goes dim . . . and then you're dead. (*Between her bursts of laughter.*) How can you *do* that? (*Sarah gets on all fours on top of* u. *dune.*) Nancy, how can you laugh when you're dead? Now, don't *do* that! (*Gets up on knees.*)

NANCY. We may be dead already, Charlie, but I think we're going to die again. Here they come! (*Leslie lunges.*)

CHARLIE. Oh my *dear* God! (*Falls back and to* l.)

NANCY. (*After a pause.*) Charlie, there's only one thing for it. Watch me now; watch me carefully. (*Sits.*)

CHARLIE. (*Gets on knees and goes to Nancy.*) Nancy . . .

NANCY. Do *this*, Charlie! For God's sake, do *this*! (*She smiles broadly; with her feet facing Leslie and Sarah, she rolls on her back, her legs drawn up, her hands by her face, fingers curved, like paws. She holds this position, smiling broadly.*)

CHARLIE. (*Confused.*) Nancy . . . (*Crawls to Nancy, pointing to Lizards.*)

NANCY. (*Sits up.*) It's called "submission," Charlie! I've seen it in the books. I've read how the animals do it. Do it, Charlie! Roll over! Please! (*Charlie hesitates a moment, looks at Leslie and Sarah.*) Do it. Charlie! (*Leslie and Sarah start to rise to their feet.*)

CHARLIE. (*Finally.*) All right. (*Both Charlie and Nancy get into submission pose.*)

NANCY. Now, Charlie, smile! And mean it!

END OF ACT ONE

ACT II

The set the same as the end of Act I. Charlie, Nancy, Leslie, and Sarah as they were. All stock still for a moment.

LESLIE. (*Turns his head toward Sarah.*) Well, Sarah, what do you think?

SARAH. (*Shakes her head.*) I don't know, Leslie.

LESLIE. What do you think they're doing?

SARAH. Well, it *looks* like some sort of a submission pose, but you never know; it might be a trick.

LESLIE. I'll take a look. (*Squats.*)

SARAH. Well, be very careful.

LESLIE. (*Rises. A weary sigh.*) Yes, Sarah. (*Leslie starts moving over to where Charlie and Nancy lie in their submission postures by going* D. R. *path and above Nancy to* C. *rock.*)

CHARLIE. Oh, my God, one of them's coming.

NANCY. Stay very still.

CHARLIE. What if one of them touches me?

NANCY. Smile.

CHARLIE. I'll scream.

NANCY. No, don't do *that*.

CHARLIE. (*Whispers out of the side of his mouth.*) It's coming! It's coming!

NANCY. Well . . . hold on, and don't panic. If we had a tail, this'd be the perfect time to wag it. (*Leslie crosses to Charlie and hits Charlie's knee with his leg. Charlie makes an involuntary sound. Leslie sniffs Charlie several times.*)

CHARLIE. Oh, God. (*Leslie stops sniffing. Charlie holds his submission pose. Leslie goes to Nancy, sniffs her a little, touches the palm of her hand. She holds submission pose. Leslie jumps over Nancy and returns to Sarah and sits* U. R. C.)

SARAH. (*Kneels* L. *of Leslie.*) Well?

LESLIE. Well . . . they don't look very . . . formidable—in the

27

sense of prepossessing. Not young. They've got their teeth bared, but they don't look as though they're going to bite. Their hide is funny—feels soft.

SARAH. How do they smell?

LESLIE. Strange.

SARAH. Well, I should suppose *so*.

LESLIE. (*Not too sure.*) I guess it's *safe*.

SARAH. Are you *sure?*

LESLIE. No; of course not. (*Nancy and Charlie are still in their submission poses.*)

NANCY. (*Sotto voce.*) What are they doing?

CHARLIE. It poked me; one of them poked me; I thought it was all over.

NANCY. (*Not to be left out.*) Well, it poked *me,* too.

CHARLIE. It *sniffed* at *me.*

NANCY. Yes. Keep where you are, Charlie; don't move. It sniffed at *me,* too.

CHARLIE. Did you smell it?

NANCY. Yes; fishy. And beautiful!

CHARLIE. Terrifying!

NANCY. (*Agreeing.*) Yes: beautiful.

LESLIE. Well, I suppose I'd better go over and . . .

SARAH. (*Immediately.*) I'll come with you.

LESLIE. (*Firmly.*) No; you stay here. (*Rises.*)

SARAH. (*Determined.*) I *said* I'll come *with* you.

LESLIE. (*Weary.*) Yes, Sarah. (*Goes to steps.*)

SARAH. There's no telling what kind of trouble you'll get yourself into. (*Rises.*)

LESLIE. Yes, Sarah. (*At top of path steps.*)

SARAH. If you're going to take *that* attitude we'd might as well . . . (*Turns to go away.*)

LESLIE. (*Rather abrupt.*) All *right,* Sarah!

SARAH. (*Feminine, submissive.*) All right, Leslie. (*Going to Leslie.*)

CHARLIE. What's happening?

NANCY. I think they're having a discussion.

LESLIE. Are you ready?

SARAH. (*Sweet.*) Yes, dear.

28

LESLIE. All right? (*Sarah nods.*) All right. (*They slowly advance toward Charlie and Nancy. Leslie crosses to c. rock and Sarah comes half-way down path ridge.*)

CHARLIE. Here they come!

NANCY. We're making history, Charlie!

CHARLIE. (*Snorts; fear and trembling.*) The sound of one hand clapping, hunh? (*Leslie goes to Charlie and raises paw to strike Charlie.*)

SARAH. (*Sitting on R. ridge.*) Don't hurt them. (*Leslie gives Sarah a disapproving look, pokes Charlie by hitting Charlie's knee with his hand.*)

CHARLIE. OW!

NANCY. (*Chiding.*) Charlie! Please!

CHARLIE. It poked me!

LESLIE. (*To Charlie as he straddles Charlie.*) Pardon me.

CHARLIE. (*To Nancy.*) What am I supposed to do if it pokes me?

LESLIE. (*Louder.*) Pardon me.

NANCY. (*Indicating Leslie.*) Speak to it, Charlie; answer it.

CHARLIE. (*Head up and on one elbow.*) Hm?

NANCY. *Speak* to it, Charlie!

CHARLIE. "Don't just lie there," you mean? (*Leslie checks Charlie's hands.*)

NANCY. I guess. (*Rolls up onto knees and waves at Sarah, tentatively.*) Hello.

SARAH. (*To Nancy.*) Hello. (*Rises. To Leslie.*) It said Hello. Did you hear it?

LESLIE. Unh-hunh. (*Investigating Charlie's feet.*)

NANCY. *Go on, Charlie.*

SARAH. Speak to the other one.

LESLIE. I've spoken to it twice; maybe it's deaf.

NANCY. *Go on.*

CHARLIE. No; then I'd have to accept it. (*Leslie looks down Charlie's pant leg.*)

SARAH. Maybe it's shy—or frightened. Try once again.

LESLIE. All right. (*Straddles Charlie again and bends down, says, rather too loudly and distinctly.*) Pardon me!

NANCY. (*Stage whisper.*) Go on, Charlie.

CHARLIE. (*Head up. Pause; then, very direct.*) Hello. (*Turns

29

to Nancy as Leslie stands up looking to Sarah.) All right? (*Back to Leslie.*) Hello! (*Brief silence as Leslie steps v. of Charlie.*)

SARAH. (*Overlapping, with Nancy's following.*) There! You see, Leslie, everything's going to be . . . (*Crosses down R. path.*)

NANCY. Good for you, Charlie! Now, that wasn't so . . . (*A growl and a raised paw from Leslie silences them both in midsentence.*)

LESLIE. Are you unfriendly?

CHARLIE. Well . . .

NANCY. Tell him, Charlie!

CHARLIE. (*Sits up and turns to Nancy, through clenched teeth.*) I'm thinking of what to say. (*Leslie goes to L. ridge rock. Turns to Leslie and his new position.*) Unfriendly? Well, no, not by nature. I'm certainly on my guard, though.

LESLIE. (*Gets on L. ridge rock.*) Yes, well, so are we.

SARAH. Indeed we are!

CHARLIE. I mean, if you're going to kill us and eat us . . . then we're unfriendly: we'll . . . resist.

LESLIE. (*Looks to Sarah for confirmation.*) Well, I certainly don't think we were planning to do *that. Were* we?

SARAH. (*None too sure.*) Well . . . no; at least I don't *think* so.

NANCY. Of *course* you weren't! The very idea! Charlie, let's introduce ourselves.

LESLIE. After all, you're rather large . . . and quite unusual. (*Afterthought.*) Were you thinking of eating *us?*

NANCY. (*Almost laughs.*) Good heavens, no!

SARAH. Well, we don't know your habits.

NANCY. I'm Nancy, and this is Charlie.

CHARLIE. How do. We don't know your habits, either. It'd be perfectly normal to assume you ate whatever . . you ran into . . . you know, whatever you ran into.

LESLIE. (*Cool.*) No; I don't know.

SARAH. (*To Nancy.*) I'm Sarah.

NANCY. Hello, Sarah.

CHARLIE. (*Somewhat on the defensive.*) It's perfectly simple: we don't eat . . . we're not cannibals.

LESLIE. What is this?

CHARLIE. Hm? We do eat other flesh . . . you know, cows, and pigs, and chickens, and all . . .

30

LESLIE. What are *they?*

CHARLIE. I guess you could put it down as a rule that we don't eat anything that . . . well, anything that *talks;* you know, English.

NANCY. (*To Charlie.*) Parrots talk; some people eat parrots.

CHARLIE. Parrots don't *talk;* parrots *imitate.* Who eats parrots?

NANCY. In the Amazon; I'm sure people eat parrots there; they're very poor, and . . .

LESLIE. What are you *saying?!*

CHARLIE. (*Frustrated.*) I'm trying to tell you . . . we don't eat our own kind.

SARAH. (*After a brief pause; flat.*) Oh.

LESLIE. (*Rather offended.*) Well, we don't eat our own kind, either. Most of us. Some.

NANCY. (*Cheerful.*) Well. You see?

LESLIE. (*Dubious.*) Well . . . (*To make the point.*) You see . . . you're *not* our kind, so you can understand the apprehension.

NANCY. Besides, we cook everything. (*Leslie crouches.*)

SARAH. Pardon?

NANCY. We cook everything, well, most things; *you* know . . . no, you don't, do you?

SARAH. This is Leslie.

NANCY. (*Extending her hand.*) How do you do, Leslie?

LESLIE. (*Regards her gesture, growls and steps over Charlie as Charlie rolls left and Leslie crosses to Nancy.*) What is that?

NANCY. Oh; we . . . well, we shake hands . . . flippers, (*Leans to Charlie.*) uh . . . Charlie?

CHARLIE. (*Gets on knees.*) When we meet we . . . take each other's hand, or whatever, and we . . . touch.

SARAH. (*Pleased.*) Oh, that's *nice.*

LESLIE. (*Not convinced.*) What for?

SARAH. (*Chiding.*) Oh, Leslie!

LESLIE. (*To Sarah, a bit piqued.*) I want to know what *for.*

CHARLIE. Well, it *used* to be, since most people are right-handed, it used to be to prove nobody had a weapon, to prove they were friendly.

LESLIE. (*After a bit.*) We're ambidextrous.

CHARLIE. (*Rather miffed.*) Well, that's *nice* for you. Very nice.

NANCY. (*To Sarah.*) And some people used to hold on to their sex parts, (*To Charlie.*) didn't you tell me that, Charlie?, that in olden times people used to hold on to their sex parts when they said hello . . . their own?

CHARLIE. (*Leans in toward Nancy.*) I don't think I told you quite that. Each other's, maybe.

NANCY. Well, no matter. (*To Leslie.*) Let's greet each other properly, all right? (*Extends her hand again.*) I give you my hand, and you give me your . . . what *is* that? What is that called? (*Indicates her arm.*)

LESLIE. What?

NANCY. (*Indicating Leslie's right arm.*) That there.

LESLIE. It's called a leg, of course.

NANCY. Oh. Well, we call this an arm.

LESLIE. You have four arms, I see. (*Indicating her arms and legs.*)

CHARLIE. No; she has two arms. (*Tiny pause.*) And two legs.

SARAH. And which are the legs?

NANCY. These here. And these are the arms.

LESLIE. (*A little on his guard.*) Why do you differentiate?

NANCY. Why do we differentiate, Charlie?

CHARLIE. (*Quietly hysterical.*) Because they're the ones with the hands on the ends of them.

NANCY. (*To Leslie.*) Yes.

SARAH. (*As Leslie glances suspiciously at Charlie.*) Go on, Leslie; do what Nancy wants you to. (*To Nancy.*) What is it called?

NANCY. Shaking hands.

CHARLIE. Or legs.

LESLIE. (*Glowers at Charlie.*) Quiet.

CHARLIE. (*Quickly.*) Yes, Sir. (*Turns away.*)

LESLIE. (*To Nancy.*) Now; what is it you want to do?

NANCY. Well . . . (*A glance at Charlie, both reassuring and imploring.*) . . . you give me your . . . that leg there, that one, and I'll give you my . . . leg, or arm, or whatever, and we'll come together by our fingers . . . these are your fingers . . . (*Wiggles fingers.*)

LESLIE. (*Wiggles his.*) Toes.

NANCY. Oh, all right; toes. (*Shakes hands with Leslie.*) And we come together like this, and we do this. (*They continue a*

32

slow, broad handshake. Leslie squats and shakes hands faster.)

LESLIE. Yes?

NANCY. And now we let go. (*They do.*) There! You see?

LESLIE. (*Somewhat puzzled about it.*) Well, that's certainly an unusual thing to want to do.

SARAH. (*Goes to Nancy, and squats leaning in.*) Let *me!* I want to! (*Sarah shakes hands with Nancy, seems happy about doing it.*) Oh, my; that's very interesting. (*Rises. To Leslie.*) Why haven't *we* ever done anything like that?

LESLIE. (*Shrugs.*) Damned if *I* know.

SARAH. (*To Leslie, referring to Charlie.*) You do it with *him,* now.

LESLIE. (*Crosses* D. C.) Are you *sure* you're friendly?

CHARLIE. (*Nervous, but serious.*) I *told* you; you'll never meet a more peaceful man. (*Leslie crosses below Charlie to* L. *ridge and Charlie goes to Nancy.*) Though of course if I thought you were going to *go* at me, or Nancy here, I'd probably defend myself . . . I mean, I *would.* (*Leslie leaps on* L. *ridge and Charlie recoils.*)

LESLIE. The danger, as *I* see it, is one of us panics. (*Charlie gives a hollow laugh.*) I think I'd like to know what frightens you. (*Charlie laughs again.*) Please?

NANCY. (*Nicely.*) Tell him, Charlie.

SARAH. Please?

CHARLIE. (*Sits up. A pause, while the nature of his questioner sinks in.*) What frightens me? Oh . . . deep space? Mortality? Nancy . . . not being with me? (*Chuckles ruefully.*) Great . . . green . . . creatures, coming up from the sea.

LESLIE. Well, that's it, you see: what we don't *know.* (*Comes down* L. *ridge going to* L. *rock*). Great, green creatures, and all, indeed! You're pretty odd yourselves, though you've probably never looked at it that way.

CHARLIE. Probably not.

LESLIE. (*Crosses* L. *ridge.*) You're not the sort of thing we run into every day.

CHARLIE. Well, *no* . . .

LESLIE. (*Points at Charlie.*) What's all *that?*

CHARLIE. (*Rises. Looks at himself.*) What?

33

LESLIE. (*Touches Charlie's shirt; says it with some distaste.*) All *that.* (*Sarah goes up on* R. *dune and sits.*)

CHARLIE. This? My shirt. (*"Naturally" implicit.*)

LESLIE. What *is* it?

NANCY. (*Rises and goes to Charlie.*) Clothes; they're called clothes; we put them on; we . . . well, we cover our skins with them.

LESLIE. Why? What for?

NANCY. Well . . . to keep warm; to look pretty; to be decent.

LESLIE. What is *that?* (*Goes up* L. *ridge to* U. L. *pinnacle. Sarah rises.*)

NANCY. Which?

LESLIE. Decent.

NANCY. Oh. Well . . . uh, not to expose our sexual parts. My breasts, for example. (*Touches them.*)

CHARLIE. Say mammaries.

NANCY. What?

SARAH. (*Goes to* R. *ridge path. Fascinated.*) What *are* they?

NANCY. Well, they (*Goes to Sarah and looks.*) . . . no, you don't seem to have them, do you? They're . . . secondary sex organs. (*Realizes it's hopeless as she says it.*) No? Well . . . (*Crosses* D. R. *beckons Sarah, begins to unbutton her blouse.*) Come here, Sarah. (*Crosses in with an eye on Leslie.*)

CHARLIE. Nancy!

NANCY. It's all *right,* Charlie. Come look, Sarah. (*Sarah crosses to Nancy.*)

SARAH. (*Bends down and peers at Nancy's open blouse.*) My gracious! Leslie, come see! (*Leslie via top ridge goes to Sarah.*)

CHARLIE. Now just a minute! (*Gets closer to Nancy.*)

NANCY. (*Laughs.*) Charlie! Don't be silly!

LESLIE. (*On* R. *ridge rock. To Charlie ingenuous.*) What's the matter?

CHARLIE. I don't want you looking at my wife's breasts, that's all.

LESLIE. I don't even know what they are.

NANCY. (*Buoyant.*) Of course not! Are you *jealous* Charlie?

CHARLIE. Of course not! How could I be jealous of . . . (*Indicates Leslie with some distaste.*) . . . how *could* I be?

34

NANCY. (*Agreeing with him.*) No.

CHARLIE. (*Reassuring himself.*) I'm *not*. (*Goes over* L *ridge to* L. *rock.*)

SARAH. (*No overtones.*) I think Leslie *should* see them.

NANCY. Yes.

LESLIE. (*To Charlie; shrugs.*) It's up to *you;* I mean if they're something you *hide* then maybe they're embarrassing, or sad, and I shouldn't *want* to see them, and . . .

CHARLIE. (*Crosses to* L. *ridge. More flustered than angry.*) They're not embarrassing; *or* sad! They're lovely! Some women . . . some women Nancy's age, they're . . . some women . . . (*To Nancy, almost spontaneously bursting into tears.*) I *love* your breasts.

NANCY. (*Gentle.*) Yes; *yes.* Thank you. (*Crossing to Charlie who sits on* L. *ridge more expansive.*) I'm not an exhibitionist, dear, as you very well know . . .

CHARLIE. . . . except that time you answered the door stark naked . . .

NANCY. (*An old story.*) We'll not discuss that now. (*To Leslie and Sarah.*) It was nothing. (*Leslie goes to top* R. *dune to above paint box.*)

CHARLIE. (*By rote.*) So *she* says.

NANCY. (*To the others.*) It was nothing; really. (*To Charlie.*) What I was trying to say, Charlie, was—and prefacing it with that I'm not an exhibitionist as you very well know—that if someone . . .

CHARLIE. (*To Nancy.*) Stark naked.

NANCY. . . . has *not* . . . has gone through life and *not* seen a woman's breasts . . . why, it's like Sarah never having seen . . . the sky. Think of the wonder of *that,* and think of the wonder of the other.

CHARLIE. (*Rather hurt.*) One of the wonders, hunh?

NANCY. I didn't *mean* it that way! (*Shakes her head; buttons up.*) Well no matter. (*Crosses to* C.)

LESLIE. (*Shrugs.*) It's up to you.

SARAH. They're really very interesting, Leslie; I'm sorry you didn't see them.

LESLIE. Well, another time, maybe.

SARAH. (*Delighted and excited.*) I suddenly remember some-

35

thing! (*Nancy sits* c. *rock.*) Leslie, do you remember when we went way north and it was very cold, and the scenery changed, and we came to the edge of a deep ravine, and all at once we heard those strange and terrible sounds . . .

LESLIE. (*Disturbed at the memory.*) Yes; I remember.

SARAH. Oh, it was a frightening set of sounds, echoing . . . all around us; and then we saw them . . . swimming by.

LESLIE. . . . enormous . . .

SARAH. Huge! Huge creatures; ten of them; maybe more; I'd never seen the size. They were of great girth.

CHARLIE. They were whales; I'm sure they were whales. (*Sarah goes to lower level* D. R. C. *and sits.*)

LESLIE. (*Goes to* R. *ridge rock.*) Is *that* what they were?

SARAH. We observed them, though, and they had young with them; young! And it was most interesting: the young would attach themselves to what I assume was the female—the mother— would attach themselves to devices that I *think* were very much like those of *yours;* resemble them.

NANCY. Of course! To the mammaries! (*Rises. Goes to* L. *of Sarah and sits* D. L. C.) Oh, Sarah, those *were* whales, for whales are mammals and they feed their young.

SARAH. Do you remember, Leslie?

LESLIE. (*Nods.*) Yes, I think I do. (*To Nancy.*) And you have those? (*Goes to Nancy and leans into Nancy as she pulls away.*) That's what *you* have? (*Charlie rises.*)

NANCY. Yes; well . . . very much like them . . . in principle.

LESLIE. (*Sits back between Sarah and Nancy.*) My gracious.

CHARLIE. (*To clear the air; brisk.*) Do you, uh . . . do *you* have any children? Any young?

SARAH. (*Laughs gaily.*) Well, of course I have! Hundreds!

CHARLIE. Hundreds!

SARAH. Certainly; I'm laying eggs all the time. (*Leslie and Sarah touch.*)

CHARLIE. (*A pause.*) You . . . lay eggs.

SARAH. Certainly! Right and left. (*A pause.*)

NANCY. Well.

LESLIE. (*Eyes narrowed.*) You, uh . . . you *don't* lay eggs, hunh?

CHARLIE. (*Incredulous.*) No; of course not!

LESLIE. (*Exploding.*) There! You see!? What did I tell you!? They don't even lay eggs! (*Goes to c. rock and sits, watchful.*)

NANCY. (*Trying to save the situation.*) How many . . . uh . . . eggs have you laid, Sarah?

SARAH. (*Thinks about it for a bit.*) Seven thousand?

NANCY. (*Admonishing.*) Oh! Sarah!

SARAH. No?

NANCY. Well, I dare say! Yes! But, really!

SARAH. I'm sorry?

NANCY. No! Never that!

CHARLIE. (*To Leslie, with some awe.*) Seven thousand! Really?

LESLIE. (*Gruff, the usual husband.*) Well, *I* don't know. I mean . . .

NANCY. (*Leans into Sarah.*) What do you *do* with them, Sarah? How do you take *care* of them?

SARAH. Well . . . they just . . . float away.

NANCY. (*Chiding.*) Oh, Sarah!

SARAH. Some get eaten—by folk passing by, which is a blessing, really, or we'd be inundated—some fall to the bottom, some catch on growing things; there's a disposition.

NANCY. Still!

SARAH. Why? What do *you* do with them?

NANCY. It's different with us, Sarah. In the birthing, I mean; I don't know about . . . well, how you go about it!

SARAH. Well (*Leans into Nancy. Shy.*) . . . we couple.

LESLIE. Shhh!

NANCY. Yes; I thought. And so do we.

SARAH. (*Relieved.*) Oh; good. And then—in a few weeks—

NANCY. Oh, it takes a lot longer for us, Sarah: nine months.

SARAH. Nine months! Leslie!

LESLIE. Wow!

SARAH. Nine months.

NANCY. And then the young are born. *Is* born . . . usually.

SARAH. Hm?

NANCY. *Is.* We usually have one, Sarah. One at a time. Oh, two, occasionally; rarely three, or more.

SARAH. Oh; Nancy!

LESLIE. (*To Charlie.*) If you have only one or two, what if they're washed away, or eaten? (*Leslie goes to Charlie and sits.*) I mean, how do you . . . perpetuate? (*Charlie rises and pulls L.*)

NANCY. (*Gay laugh.*) That never happens, we keep them with us . . . 'till they're all grown up and ready for the world.

SARAH. How long is that?

CHARLIE. Eighteen . . . twenty years.

LESLIE. (*A slight pause.*) You're not serious!

NANCY. Oh, yes, we *are!*

LESLIE. You *can't* be.

CHARLIE. (*Defensive.*) Why not?

LESLIE. Well . . . I mean . . . *think* about it.

CHARLIE. (*Does.*) Well . . . it *is* a long time, all right, but there's no other way for it.

NANCY. Just as you let them float away, or get caught on things; there's no other way for it.

SARAH. How many have you birthed?

NANCY. Three.

LESLIE. Pft! (*Gets on all fours.*)

SARAH. (*Still with the wonder of that.*) Only three.

NANCY. Of course, there's *another* reason we keep them with us.

SARAH. Oh? What is that?

NANCY. (*Puzzled at her question.*) Well . . . we *love* them.

LESLIE. Pardon?

CHARLIE. We *love* them.

LESLIE. (*Turns to Charlie and sits on haunches.*) Explain.

CHARLIE. What?

LESLIE. What you said.

CHARLIE. We said we love them.

LESLIE. Yes; explain.

CHARLIE. (*Incredulous.*) What *love* means!?

NANCY. (*To Sarah.*) Love? Love is one of the emotions. (*They look at her, waiting.*) One of the *emotions,* Sarah.

SARAH. (*After a tiny pause.*) But, what *are* they?!

NANCY. (*Becoming impatient.*) Well, you *must* have them. You *must* have *emotions.* (*Rises. Crosses U. R.*)

LESLIE. (*Sits. Quite impatient.*) We may, or we may not, but we'll never know unless you define your terms. Honestly, the imprecision! You're so thoughtless! (*Sarah goes to Leslie.*)

CHARLIE. (*Miffed.*) Well, we're sorry!

LESLIE. You have to make allowances!

CHARLIE. All *right!!*

LESLIE. Just . . . thoughtless.

CHARLIE. All *right!*

SARAH. (*Crawls toward Nancy.*) *Help* us, Nancy.

NANCY. (*To Sarah and Leslie.*) Fear. Hatred. Apprehension. Loss. Love. (*Pause.*) Nothing? (*A bedtime story with Sarah and Leslie listening.*) We keep them with us because they need us to —and we feel possessive toward them, and grateful, and proud . . .

CHARLIE. (*Ironic.*) And lots of *other* words describing emotions. You can't *do* that, Nancy; it doesn't help.

NANCY. (*Annoyed.*) All right. Then *you* do it! (*Using path steps she goes to* R. *ridge rock and sits.*) And when we get back home, I'm packing up and taking a good long trip. *Alone.* I've been married to you far too smoothly for far too long.

CHARLIE. (*To Leslie.*) That's an example of emotion: frustration, anger . . .

NANCY. (*To herself.*) I'm too *old* to have an affair. (*Pause.*) *No,* I'm not. (*Pause.*) *Yes* I am.

CHARLIE. (*Chuckling.*) Oh, come on, Nancy. (*To Leslie and Sarah.*) Maybe *I* can do it. (*Leslie and Sarah turn to Charlie to listen.*) How did you two get together? How'd ya meet?

LESLIE. Well, I was just going along, one day, minding my own business . . . (*Crawling* L.)

SARAH. Oh, Leslie! (*Crawls* D. R. C. *to Charlie.*) I was reaching my maturity, and so, naturally, (*Leslie crawls to in front of Sarah keeping low.*) a lot of males were paying attention to me—milling around—you know—preening and snapping at each other and generally showing off, and I noticed one was hanging around a little distance away, not joining in with the others . . .

LESLIE. That was me.

SARAH. . . . and I didn't pay too much attention to him, because I thought he was probably sickly, or something, (*Leslie circles Sarah, getting* L. *of Sarah.*) and besides, there were so many others, and it was time to start coupling . . .

LESLIE. *You* noticed me.

SARAH. . . . when, all of a sudden! There he was, right in the

39

middle of them, snapping away, really fighting, driving all the others off. It was quite a rumpus.

LESLIE. (*An aside, to Charlie.*) They didn't *amount* to much.

SARAH. (*Shrugs.*) And so . . . all the others drifted away . . . and there he was.

LESLIE. They didn't *drift* away: I drove them away. (*Lies flat.*)

SARAH. Well, I suppose that's true. (*Bright.*) Show them your scar, Leslie! (*To Charlie and Nancy.*) Leslie has a marvelous scar!

LESLIE (*Proud.*) Oh . . . some other time.

SARAH. And there he *was* . . . and there *I* was . . . and here we *are.*

CHARLIE. Well, yes! That proves my point!

LESLIE. (*Rolls body to* R.) What? (*Pause.*)

CHARLIE. About *love.* (*Pause.*) He *loved* you.

SARAH. Yes?

CHARLIE. Well, *yes.* He drove the others away so he could have *you.* He wanted *you.*

SARAH. (*As if what Charlie has said proves nothing.*) Ye-es?

CHARLIE. Well . . . it's so *clear.* Nancy, isn't it clear!? (*Stepping to* L. *ridge.*)

NANCY. I don't *know.* Don't talk to me; you're a terrible person.

CHARLIE. (*Under his breath.*) Oh, for God's sake! Leslie! (*Leslie pulls* U. L. *and sits on blanket.*) *Why* did you want Sarah?

LESLIE. Well, as I told you: I was just going along one day, minding my own business, and there was this great commotion, with all the others around her, and so I decided *I* wanted her.

CHARLIE. (*Losing, but game.*) Didn't you think she was . . . pretty—or whatever?

LESLIE. I couldn't really see, with all the others hovering. She *smelled* all right.

CHARLIE. Have you ever, you know . . . coupled with anyone else since you met Sarah?

NANCY. Charlie!

LESLIE. (*Pause; too defensive.*) Why should I?

CHARLIE. (*Smiles.*) Just asking. (*Patient.*) Is that your *nature?* Not to go around coupling whenever you feel like it, whatever female strikes your fancy.

SARAH. (*Fascinated.*) *Very* interesting.

LESLIE. (*To shut her up.*) It is *not!* (*To Charlie.*) I've coupled in my time. (*Crawling to* D. L. *ridge rock.*)

CHARLIE. Since you met Sarah?

LESLIE. I'm not going to *answer* that. (*Pulls* U. L.)

SARAH. (*Hurt.*) You *have?*

CHARLIE. No; he means he hasn't. And he's embarrassed by it. What about you, Sarah? Have you been with anyone since Leslie?

LESLIE. Of *course* she hasn't!

NANCY. (*Rises.*) What an *awful* question to ask Sarah! You should be *ashamed* of yourself!

CHARLIE. It's not an awful question at all.

NANCY. It *is!* It's dreadful! Of course she hasn't.

CHARLIE. (*Annoyed.*) What *standards* are you using? How would *you* know?

NANCY. (*Up on her high horse.*) I just know.

CHARLIE. Things might be different, you know . . . (*Gestures vaguely around.*) . . . down . . . *there.* I don't think it's dreadful at *all.*

SARAH. (*To Nancy and Charlie.*) The truth of the matter is: no, I haven't.

LESLIE. What are you getting at!?

CHARLIE. It's hard to explain!

LESLIE. Apparently.

CHARLIE. Especially to someone who has no grasp of conceptual matters, who hasn't heard of half the words in the English language, who lives on the bottom of the sea and has green scales! (*Goes to* L. *rock.*)

LESLIE. Look, buddy . . . !

SARAH. Leslie . . . (*Goes to Leslie and touches him.*) NANCY. Now you two boys just . . .

CHARLIE. (*Half to himself.*) Might as well be talking to a fish. (*Getting on* L. *rock.*)

LESLIE. (*Crosses* L. C. *and sits. Really angry.*) That does it!

NANCY. Charlie! Look out! (*Charlie turns.*) Sarah, stop him!

SARAH. (*Stays with Leslie.*) Leslie! You be nice!

LESLIE. (*To Sarah.*) He called me a fish!

SARAH. He did not!

NANCY. No he didn't; not quite. He said he might as well.

LESLIE. Same thing.

41

CHARLIE. (*A glint in his eye.*) Oh? What's the matter with fish?

NANCY. Calm down, Charlie . . .

CHARLIE. (*Persisting.*) What's the matter with fish, hunh?

SARAH. Be good, Leslie . . .

LESLIE. (*Rises. Crosses to L. ridge. On his high horse—so to speak.*) We just don't think very highly of fish, that's all.

CHARLIE. (*Seeing a triumph somewhere.*) Oh? You don't like fish, hunh?

NANCY. Now, *both* of you!

CHARLIE. What's the matter with fish all of a sudden?

LESLIE. (*Real middle-class, but not awful.*) For one thing, there're too many of them; they're all over the place . . . racing around, darting in front of you, picking at everything . . . moving in, taking over where you live . . . and they're stupid! (*Crosses to C.*)

SARAH. (*Rises, crosses R. C. Shy.*) Not all of them; porpoises aren't stupid.

LESLIE. (*Turns to Sarah. Still wound up.*) All right! Except for porpoises . . . they're stupid! (*To Charlie. Thinks about it some more.*) And they're dirty.

CHARLIE. (*Mouth opens in amazement and delight.*) You're . . . you're prejudiced! Nancy, he's . . . you're a bigot! (*Laughs.*) You're a goddamn bigot!

LESLIE. (*Gets on L. ridge. Dangerous.*) Yeah? What's that?

NANCY. Be careful, Charlie.

LESLIE. (*Not amused.*) What *is* that?

CHARLIE. What? A bigot?

LESLIE. I don't know. Is that what you said?

CHARLIE. (*Right on with it.*) A bigot is somebody who thinks he's better than somebody else because they're different.

LESLIE. (*Brief pause; anger defused.*) Oh; well, then; that's all right. I'm not what you said. It's *not* because they're different: it's because they're stupid and they're dirty and they're all over the place! (*Goes to C. and sits.*)

CHARLIE. (*Parody of studying and accepting.*) Oh. Well. That's all right, then. (*Turns away.*)

NANCY. (*Wincing some.*) Careful, Charlie.

LESLIE. (*Absorbed with his own words.*) Being different is . . .

42

interesting; there's nothing implicitly inferior or superior about it. *Great* difference, of course, produces natural caution; and if the differences are too extreme . . . well, then, reality tends to fade away.

NANCY. (*An aside; to Charlie.*) And so much for conceptual matters.

CHARLIE. (*Dismissing it with bravado.*) Ooooooooo, he probably read it somewhere. (*Crosses away.*)

SARAH. (*Looks at the sky, and about her, expansively.*) My! It *is* quite something out here, isn't it? You can see! So very far! (*She sees birds with some consternation.*) What are those? (*Leslie sees them. Tenses. Does an intake of breath.*)

NANCY. (*Looking up.*) Birds. Those are birds, Sarah. (*Leslie, in reaction to the birds, growls, starts moving up the rock ridge, L.*)

SARAH. (*Goes up path steps.*) Leslie! Leslie! (*Leslie continues to move up to top of the rock U. L. pinnacle. Nancy and Charlie meet L. C. in fear.*)

NANCY. What is he doing?

SARAH. Well, he . . . he does it everywhere we go, so why not up here? He checks things out, makes sure a way is open for us . . .

CHARLIE. (*Turns front.*) It's called instinct.

SARAH. (*Politely but not terribly interested.*) Oh? *Is* it?

CHARLIE. (*Nods; quite happy.*) Instinct.

SARAH. Well, this isn't the sort of situation we run into every day, *and* . . . creatures do tend to be devious: you don't know what's going to happen from one minute to the next . . .

NANCY. Certainly, certainly. Will he be all right? I mean . . .

SARAH. (*Crosses down path ridge.*) Oh, certainly. He's kind and he's a good mate, and when he tells me what we're going to do, I find I can live with it quite nicely. And you?

NANCY. Uh . . . well, we manage rather like that I guess.

SARAH. (*Rapt looking L. and up.*) Oh, my goodness. *See* them up there! How they *go!*

CHARLIE. Seagulls.

SARAH. Sea . . . gulls. The wonder of it! What holds them up?

CHARLIE. (*Shy, but helpful.*) Aerodynamics.

SARAH. (*Still enraptured.*) Indeed.

NANCY. Oh, really, Charlie!

CHARLIE. (*Feelings hurt.*) Well, it *is*.

SARAH. (*To him.*) Oh, I wasn't *doubting* it. (*Attention back to birds.*) See them swim!

CHARLIE. (*More sure of himself now.*) Fly, they fly; birds fly.

SARAH. (*Watching the birds.*) The rays are rather like that: swimming about; what do you call it—flying. Funny creatures; shy, really; don't give that impression, though; standoffish, rather curt.

NANCY. (*Sits.*) Rays. Yes; well, we know them.

SARAH. (*Sits. Pleased.*) *Do* you!

CHARLIE. Nancy means we've *seen* them; photographs.

NANCY. Yes. In photographs.

SARAH. What is *that*?

CHARLIE. Photographs? It's a . . . no, I'd better not try.

SARAH. (*Coquettish.*) Something I shouldn't know? Something you could tell Leslie but not me?

NANCY. (*Laughs.*) Heavens no!

SARAH. I mean, I *am* a married woman.

CHARLIE. (*Surprised.*) Do you do *that*? I mean, do you . . . ? I don't know what I mean.

NANCY. Charlie! Just think what we can tell our children and our grandchildren: that we were here when Sarah saw it all!

CHARLIE. Sure! And if you think they'd have us put away for all that other—for living on the beach . . .

NANCY. (*Nodding along.*) . . . "from beach to beach, seaside nomads . . ."

CHARLIE. (*Kneels* L. *of Nancy.*) . . . yes, then *what* do you *think* they'd *say* about *this!* (*Mimics her.*) "Charlie and I were sitting around, you see, when all at once, lo and behold, these two great green lizards . . . " How do you think they'd take to *that*? Put it in one of your postcards, Nancy, and mail it out.

NANCY. Ohhhhh, Charlie! You give me the pip, you know that?

SARAH. (*Rises. Goes up* U. R. *ridge path. Calling to Leslie.*) Leslie, Leslie.

LESLIE. (*Turns to Sarah.*) Are you all right?

SARAH. Oh Leslie, I've had an absolutely fascinating time. Leslie . . . up *there?*

LESLIE. What *are* they?

44

SARAH. (*Bubbling with it.*) They're called *birds,* and they don't swim, they fly, and they stay up by something called aerodynamics . . .

LESLIE. What is *that?*

SARAH. (*Rushing on.*) I'm sure I don't know, and I said they looked like rays, and *they* said they knew rays through something called photographs, though they wouldn't tell me what that *was,* and Charlie gives Nancy the pip.

LESLIE. There, I was right!! You can't trust somebody like that! How can you trust somebody like that? (*Goes to Sarah via top ridge. Sarah moves half way down R. ridge path where Leslie meets her.*) You can't trust somebody like that!

NANCY. (*With a desperate attempt to save the situation.*) Well, what does it matter? We're all *dead.*

SARAH. Dead? Who's dead?

NANCY. *We* are.

SARAH. (*Disbelief.*) No.

NANCY. According to Charlie here.

CHARLIE. (*Without humor.*) It's not to be joked about.

SARAH. *All* of us?

NANCY. (*Chuckles.*) Well, I'm not certain about that; (*Charlie sits.*) he and I, apparently. It all has to do with liver paste. The fatal sandwich. (*Leslie and Sarah look at each other.*)

CHARLIE. Explain it right! Leave it alone if you're not going to give it the dignity it deserves.

NANCY. (*To Leslie and Sarah; a trifle patronizing.*) Well, I mean we *have* to be dead because Charlie has decided that the wonders do not occur; that what we have not known does not exist; (*Leslie crawls slowly to U. L. top pinnacle via top ridge.*) that what we cannot fathom cannot be; that the miracles, if you will, are bedtime stories; he has taken the leap of faith, from agnostic to atheist; the world is flat; the sun and the planets revolve about it, and don't row out too far or you'll fall off.

CHARLIE. (*Sad; embarrassed.*) I couldn't live with you again; I'm glad it doesn't matter.

NANCY. (*To Charlie; nicely.*) Oh, Charlie.

LESLIE. (*To Charlie, not believing any of it.*) When did you die? (*Gets on U. L. rock step.*)

45

CHARLIE. Pardon?

SARAH. (*Comes down* R. *ridge path on bended knee, to Nancy; whispering.*) He's not dead.

NANCY. (*To Sarah.*) I know.

LESLIE. Did we frighten you to death, or was it before we met you?

CHARLIE. Oh, *before* we met you; after lunch.

LESLIE. Then I take it *we* don't *exist.*

CHARLIE. (*Apologetic.*) Probably not; I'm sorry.

LESLIE. (*To Nancy.*) That's quite a mind he's got there.

NANCY. (*Grudgingly defending Charlie.*) Well . . . he thinks things through. (*Very cheerful.*) As for *me,* I couldn't care less: I'm having far too interesting a time.

SARAH. (*Gets on all fours.*) Oh, I'm so glad!

LESLIE. (*Comes three steps down* L. *ridge. Puzzled.*) I *think* I exist.

CHARLIE. (*Shrugs.*) Well, *that's* all that matters; it's the same thing.

NANCY. (*To Sarah; considerable enthusiasm.*) Oh, a voice from the dead.

LESLIE. (*To Charlie.*) You mean it's all an illusion?

CHARLIE. (*More interested in the other conversation.*) Could be.

LESLIE. The whole thing? Existence?

CHARLIE. Unh-hmhm!

LESLIE. (*Leaps to next to Charlie's left.*) I don't believe *that* at all.

CHARLIE. (*Rises up on knees.*) Well, it isn't *my* theory.

LESLIE. Whose theory *is* it, then?

CHARLIE. (*Angry.*) What?!

LESLIE. Whose theory *is* it? Don't you yell at me.

CHARLIE. I am not *yelling* at you!

LESLIE. *Yes,* you are! You *did!*

CHARLIE. Well, then, I'm sorry.

LESLIE. Whose *theory* is it?

CHARLIE. (*Weary.*) Descartes.

LESLIE. (*Annoyed.*) What is *that?*

CHARLIE. What?

LESLIE. What you *said.*

CHARLIE. (*Barely in control.*) DESCARTES!! DESCARTES!!
I THINK: THEREFORE I AM!! (*Pause.*) COGITO! ERGO!
SUM! I THINK: THEREFORE I AM!! (*Pause. Pleading.*)
Now you're going to ask me what *think* means. (*Leslie goes up*
L. *ridge.*)
NANCY. (*Comforting, leaning to him, genuine.*) No, he's *not;*
he wouldn't *do* that.
CHARLIE. I haven't got it *in* me.
NANCY. It's all right. (*Touches Charlie.*)
LESLIE. (*To Sarah.*) *I* know what think means.
SARAH. Of course you do!
LESLIE. (*Agreeing.*) Well!
CHARLIE. I couldn't take it.
NANCY. It's not going to happen.
CHARLIE. It's more than I could . . . death is release, if you've
lived all right, and *I* have. (*Sits cross-legged.*) As well as most,
easily; when it comes time, and I put down my fork on the plate,
line it up with the knife, take a last sip of wine, or water, touch
my lips and fold the napkin, push back the chair . . .
NANCY. (*Shakes him by the shoulders, looks him in the eye.*)
Oh, Charlie! (*Sarah and Leslie watch and lean in while Nancy
kisses him on the mouth, her tongue entering, for quite a little;
he is passive, then slowly responds, taking comfort, and sharing;
they come apart, finally; he shrugs, chuckles timidly, smiles.*)
CHARLIE. (*Shy.*) Well.
NANCY. It is all *right.* You're alive, and it's all *right.* And, if it
isn't . . . well, it will just have to do. No matter *what.*
CHARLIE. (*Irony.*) And this will have to do?
NANCY. Yes. This will have to do.
SARAH. (*Crawl two steps in.*) Is he all right?
NANCY. Well, you see . . . he's been through life you see, and
yes, I suppose he's all right. (*The sound of the jet plane again
from* L. *growing, becoming deafeningly loud, diminishing. Charlie
and Nancy follow its course; Nancy rises and goes to path steps.
Leslie and Sarah are terrified; they rush half out of sight over
the dune. Sarah* D. R. *lying flat on stomach, legs only visible—
Leslie scampers into* U. L. *cove. Nancy, in the silence following the
plane.*) Such *noise* they make.

CHARLIE. They'll crash into the dunes one day; I don't know what good they do.

NANCY. (*Seeing Leslie and Sarah, pointing to them.*) Oh, Charlie! Look! Look at them!

CHARLIE. Hm? What? (*Gets up on knees. Sees them.*) Oh!

NANCY. (*Crosses* D. R.) Oh, Charlie; they're frightened. They're so frightened!

CHARLIE. (*Awe.*) Yes. They are.

LESLIE. (*Crossing to* L. R. *ridge, from where he is; calling.*) What *was* that!?

NANCY. (*Calling; a light tone.*) It was an aeroplane.

LESLIE. Well, what *is* it?! (*Crawling up* L. *ridge to* U. L. *top pinnacle and down top ridge to Sarah. Charlie and Nancy come together* C.)

CHARLIE. It's a machine that . . . it's a method of . . . (*Sarah goes to* R. *ridge path where she meets Leslie crouching.*)

LESLIE. What?

CHARLIE. (*Shouting.*) It's a machine that . . . it's a method of . . . it's a . . . it's like a bird, except that we make them—we put them together, and we get inside them and that's how we fly . . . sort of.

SARAH. (*Some awe.*) It's terrifying!

NANCY. Well, you get used to it.

LESLIE. (*To Charlie; to get it straight.*) You . . . fly.

CHARLIE. Yes. Well, some do. *I* have. Yes! *I* fly. We do all sorts of things up here.

LESLIE. I'll bet you do.

CHARLIE. Sure; give us a machine and there isn't anywhere we don't go. Why, we even have a machine that will . . . go down there; under water.

LESLIE. (*Leaps to* D. R. *Brow furrowed.*) Then . . . you've *been* —what do you call it: under water?

CHARLIE. Well, not in one of the machines, no. And nowhere near as deep.

NANCY. Charlie *used* to go under—near the shore, of course; not very deep.

CHARLIE. Oh, God . . . years ago.

NANCY. Yes, and Charlie has missed it. He was telling me how much he used to love to go down under, settle on the bottom, wait for the fish to come . . .

CHARLIE. (*Embarrassed; indicating Leslie and Sarah.*) It was a *long* time ago. (*To Nancy.*) Nancy, not now! Please!

LESLIE (*Very interested.*) *Really*

CHARLIE. It didn't *amount* to much.

NANCY. Oh, it *did;* it *did* amount, and to a great deal.

CHARLIE. (*Embarrassed and angry.*) Lay off, Nancy!

NANCY. (*Turns on Charlie, impatient and angry.*) It used to make you *happy,* and you used to be *proud* of what made you happy!

CHARLIE. (*Goes to L. rock.*) LEAVE OFF!! (*Subsides.*) Just . . . leave off. (*Nancy crosses to L. ridge. A silence. Now, to Leslie and Sarah; quietly.*) It was just a game; it was enough for a twelve-year-old, maybe, but it wasn't . . . finding out, you know; it wasn't *real.* It wasn't enough for a memory. (*Sits L. rock and Nancy sits three quarters up L. ridge. Pause; shakes his head. Barely controlled rage; to Leslie.*) Why did you come up here in the first place?

LESLIE. (*Goes to C. rock. Too matter-of-fact.*) I don't know.

CHARLIE. (*Thunder.*) COME! ON!

LESLIE. I don't know! (*To Sarah; too off-hand.*) *Do* I know?

SARAH. (*Rises. Yes and no.*) Well . . .

LESLIE. (*Final.*) No, I don't know.

SARAH. (*Goes to Leslie, touching paw.*) We had a sense of not belonging anymore.

LESLIE. Don't Sarah.

SARAH. (*Gets on all fours, D. C.*) I should, Leslie. It was a growing thing, nothing abrupt, nor that anything was different for that matter.

LESLIE. (*Helpless.*) Don't go on, Sarah.

SARAH. . . . in the sense of having changed; but . . . *we* had changed . . . (*Looks about her.*) . . . all of a sudden, everything . . . down there . . . was terribly . . . interesting, I suppose; but what did it have to do with *us* anymore?

LESLIE. Don't, Sarah.

SARAH. And it wasn't . . . comfortable anymore. I mean, after all, you make your nest, and accept a whole . . . array . . . of

49

things . . . and . . . we didn't feel we *belonged* there anymore. And . . . what were we going to do?!

CHARLIE. (*After a little; shy.*) And that's why you came up.

LESLIE. We talked about it.

SARAH. Yes. We did for a long time. Considered the pros and the cons. Making do down there or trying something else. But what?

CHARLIE. And so you came up.

LESLIE. Is that what we did? Is that what we were doing? I don't know.

CHARLIE. (*He has hardly been listening; speaks to himself more than to anyone else.*) All that time; the eons.

LESLIE. Hm?

NANCY. What was that, Charlie?

CHARLIE. The eons. How long is an eon?

NANCY. (*Encouraging him.*) A very long time.

CHARLIE. A hundred million years? Ten times that? Well, a distance, certainly. What do they call it . . . the primordial soup? the glop? That heartbreaking second when it all got together, the sugars and the acids and the ultraviolets, and the next thing you knew there were tangerines and string quartets.

LESLIE. (*Crawls* L. C.) What are *they*?

CHARLIE. (*Smiles, a little sadly, shrugs.*) It doesn't matter. But somewhere in all that time, halfway, probably, halfway between the aminos and the treble clef—(*Leslie turns to Sarah. Crosses to* L. *ridge on knee. Directed to Sarah and Leslie.*)—listen to this— there was a time when we *all* were down there, crawling around, and swimming and carrying on—remember how we read about it, Nancy . . .

NANCY. Yes . . . crawling around, and swimming . . . rather like it is now, but very different.

CHARLIE. Yes; very. (*To Leslie and Sarah.*) Are you interested in any of this?

SARAH. (*Genuine, and pert.*) Oh! Fascinated!

CHARLIE. And you understand it; I mean, you follow it.

LESLIE. (*Hurt, if not quite sure of himself.*) Of *course* we follow it.

SARAH. (*Wavering a little.*) Of . . . of course.

NANCY. Of *course* they do.

50

LESLIE. *(A kind of bluff.)* "Rather like it is now, but very different" ... *(Shrugs.)* Whatever that means.

CHARLIE. *(Enthusiastic didacticism.)* It means that once upon a time you and I lived down there.

LESLIE. Oh, come on!

CHARLIE. Well, no, not literally, and *not* you and me, for that matter, but what we became.

LESLIE. *(Feigning enthusiastic belief.)* Unh-hunh; unh-hunh. *(Crawling R.)*

SARAH. *(Crawls to Charlie.)* When were we all down there?

CHARLIE. Oh, a long time ago. *(Sits on L. rock.)*

NANCY. Once upon a time, Sarah.

SARAH. *(During pause Sarah crawls R. of L. ridge facing Nancy. Leslie crawls to C. rock.)* Yes?

NANCY. *(Laughs, realizing she is supposed to continue.)* Oh, my goodness. I feel silly.

CHARLIE. Why? All you're going to do is explain evolution to a couple of lizards.

NANCY. *(Leslie lies head on C. rock. Nancy, rising above it.)* Once upon a time, Sarah, a long, long time ago, long before you were born — even before Charlie, here, was born ...

CHARLIE. *(Feigning great boredom.)* Veeeerrry funny.

NANCY. Nothing was like it is at all today. There were fish, but they didn't look like any fish you've ever seen.

SARAH. My goodness!

LESLIE. What happened to them?

NANCY. *(Trying to find it exactly.)* Well ... they were dissatisfied, is what they were. So, they grew, or diminished, or ... or sprouted things — tails, spots, fins, feathers.

SARAH. It sounds extremely busy.

NANCY. Well, it *was*. Of course, it didn't happen all at once.

SARAH. *(Looks to Leslie.)* Oh?

NANCY. *(A pleased laugh.)* Oh, *heavens* no. Small changes; adding up. Like ... well, there probably was a time when Leslie didn't have a tail. *(Leslie sits up.)*

SARAH. *(Laughs.)* Oh, really!

LESLIE. Quite dry.) I've always had a tail.

NANCY. *(Bright.)* Oh, no; there was a time, way back, you didn't. Before you needed it you didn't have one.

LESLIE. (*Rises with tail in hand. Through his teeth.*) I have *always* had a *tail*. (*Stroking his tail.*)

SARAH. Leslie's very proud of his tail, Nancy . . .

CHARLIE. You like your tail, do you?

LESLIE. I have *always* had a *tail*.

SARAH. (*Crawls one step to Leslie.*) Of course you have, Leslie; it's a lovely tail.

LESLIE. (*Hugging his tail in front of him; anxiety on his face.*) I have. I've always had one.

NANCY. (*Trying again.*) Well, of course, you have, and so did your father before you, and his, too, I have no doubt, and so on back, but maybe they had a smaller tail than you, or a larger.

LESLIE. Smaller!

SARAH. Leslie's extremely proud of his tail; it's very large and sturdy and . . .

NANCY. Well, I'm sure; yes.

LESLIE. (*Eyeing Charlie.*) *You* don't have a tail.

CHARLIE. (*Rather proud.*) No, I don't.

LESLIE. What happened to it?

CHARLIE. It fell off. (*Leslie gets on all fours* D. R.—*Sarah turns front.*) Mutate or perish. Let your tail drop off, change your spots or maybe just your point of view. The dinosaurs . . . they knew a thing or two, but that was about it . . . great, enormous creatures, big as a diesel engine—(*Leslie stirs. To Leslie.*)—whatever that may be—Leviathans! . . . with a brain the size of a lichee nut; couldn't cope; couldn't figure it all out; went down.

LESLIE. (*Quite disgusted.*) What are you talking about?

CHARLIE. Just running on, and trying to make a point. (*Rises.*) And do you know what happened once? Kind of the crowning moment of it all for me? It was when some . . . slimy creature poked his head out of the muck, looked around and decided to spend some time up here . . . came up into the air and decided to stay? And as time went on, he split apart and evolved and became tigers and gazelles and porcupines and Nancy, here . . . (*Sarah turns to Nancy—Nancy nods in agreement. Sarah crawls to* C. *rock.*)

LESLIE. (*Crawls* R. *Annoyed.*) I don't believe a word of this!

CHARLIE. Oh, you'd better, for he went back under, too; part of what he became didn't fancy it up on land, and went back down

52

there, and turned into porpoises and sharks, and Manta rays and whales . . . and you.

LESLIE. Come off it!

CHARLIE. It's called flux. And it's always going on; right now, to all of us. (*Crosses* U. L. *two steps.*)

SARAH. (*Shy.*) Is it . . . is it for the better?

CHARLIE. Is it for the *better*? I don't *know*. Progress is a set of assumptions. It's very beautiful down there. It's all still, and the fish float by. It's very beautiful.

LESLIE. Don't get taken in.

CHARLIE. What are you going to tell me about. Slaughter . . . pointlessness? Come on *up* here. *Stay.* (*Looks to Nancy.*) The optimists say you mustn't look just yet, that it's all going to work out fine, no matter *what* you've heard; the pessimists, on the other hand . . .

NANCY. It *is*. It all *is*.

CHARLIE. (*Slightly mocking.*) Why!?

NANCY. Because I couldn't bear to think of it otherwise, that's why. I'm not one of these people says that I'm better than a . . . a rabbit; just that I'm more interesting: I use tools, I make art . . . (*Turning introspective.*) . . . and I'm aware of my own mortality. (*Pause.*) Very. (*Pouting; very much like a little girl.*) All rabbits do is eat carrots.

SARAH. (*To Charlie; after a little pause; sotto voce.*) What are carrots?

CHARLIE. (*Shrugs it off; not interested.*) Oh . . . something you eat. They make noise.

LESLIE. (*Curiously bitter.*) And tools; and art; and mortality? Do you eat *them*? And do *they* make a noise?

CHARLIE. (*Staring hard at Leslie.*) Yeah, they make a noise.

NANCY. (*She, too.*) What is it, Leslie?

LESLIE. (*Intense and angry.*) What *are* these things!?

NANCY. Tools; art; mortality?

CHARLIE. They're what separate *us* from the brute beast. (*Leslie stirs.*)

NANCY. (*Very quiet.*) No, Charlie; don't.

LESLIE. (*Quiet, cold, and formal.*) You'll have to forgivé me, but what is "brute beast"?

NANCY. Charlie; no!

CHARLIE. (*Defiant.*) Brute beast?

LESLIE. (*Goes up steps to top. Grim.*) I don't like the sound of it.

CHARLIE. (*Stares right at him.*) Brute beast? It's not even aware it's *alive* much less it's going to die!

LESLIE. (*Rises. Pause; then as if to memorize the words.*) Brute. Beast. Yes?

CHARLIE. Right on. (*Pause.*)

LESLIE. (*Suddenly aware of all eyes on him.*) Stop it! Stop it! What are you looking at? Why don't you mind your own business? (*Turns away and sits, curling tail into him.*)

NANCY. What more do you want?

CHARLIE. (*Intense.*) I don't *know* what more I want. (*To Leslie and Sarah.*) I don't know what I want for *you.* I don't know what I feel toward you; it's either love or loathing. Take your pick; they're both emotions. And you're finding out about them, aren't you? About emotions? Well, I want you to know about *all* of it; I'm impatient for you. I want you to experience the whole thing! The full sweep! Maybe I envy you . . . down *there,* free from it all; down there with the *beasts?* (*A pause.*) What would you do, Sarah? . . . if Leslie went away . . . for a long time . . . what would you do then?

SARAH. (*Crawls to* R. C.) If he didn't tell me where he was going?

CHARLIE. If he'd gone! (*Under his breath.*) For God's sake. (*Back. Gets on bended knee.*) If he'd taken off, and you hadn't seen him for the *longest* time.

SARAH. I'd go look for him.

LESLIE. (*Crawls on top ridge* U. R. C. *Suspicious.*) What are you after?

CHARLIE. (*To Sarah; ignoring Leslie.*) You'd go look for him; fine. But what if you knew he was never coming back? (*Sarah does a sharp intake of breath as she crawls* D. R.) What about that?

NANCY. You're heartless, Charlie; you're relentless and without heart.

CHARLIE. (*Eyes narrowing.*) What would you do, Sarah? (*A pause, then she begins to sob.*)

SARAH. I'd . . . I'd . . .

CHARLIE. You'd cry; you'd cry your eyes out.

SARAH. I'd . . . cry; I'd . . . I'd cry! I'd . . . I'd cry my eyes out! Oh . . . Leslie!

LESLIE. (*Trying to comfort Sarah.*) It's all right, Sarah!

SARAH. I want to go back; I don't want to stay here anymore. (*Wailing as she goes up D. R. dune—Leslie crawls to U. L. pinnacle circling in place.*) I want to go *back!* I want to go *back!*

NANCY. (*Moves to Sarah to comfort her.*) Oh, now, Sarah! Please!

SARAH. (*Bursts into new sobbing.*) Oh, Nancy! I want to go *back.*

NANCY. Sarah!

CHARLIE. (*Crossing to Sarah.*) I'm sorry; I'm . . . I'm sorry.

LESLIE. (*Getting one foot on U. L. rock step.*) Hey! Mister! (*Charlie turns to Leslie.*) You've made her cry; she's never done anything like that before. You made her cry!

CHARLIE. I'm sorry.

LESLIE. (*Comes stalkingly to Charlie.*) You made her cry! (*Hits Charlie sending him down on the sand.*) I ought to tear you apart! (*Grabs Charlie, pulls him up on his feet and begins to choke Charlie, standing behind Charlie, his arms around Charlie's throat. It has the look of slow, massive inevitability, not fight and panic.*)

CHARLIE. Oh, my God!

NANCY. Charlie!

SARAH. Leslie! Stop it!

NANCY. Stop! Please!

SARAH. Leslie!

CHARLIE. Help . . . me . . .

LESLIE. (*Straining with the effort.*) You . . . made . . . her . . . cry . . . mister. (*Leslie suddenly lets go; Charlie sinks to the sand landing D. R. C.—Nancy runs to Charlie.*)

NANCY. Oh, my God!

LESLIE. Don't you talk to me about brute beast. (*There is a slight pause.*)

SARAH. (*To Leslie.*) See to him.

LESLIE. (*Goes to L. ridge.*) Are you all right?

CHARLIE. Yes; yes, I am. (*Slowly sits up, Nancy still with him. Pause.*)

LESLIE. (*Crosses to L. rock-sits.*) It's . . . rather dangerous . . . up here.

CHARLIE. Everywhere.

LESLIE. Well. I think we'll go back down now.

NANCY. No!

LESLIE. Oh, yes. I think we must.

NANCY. (*Rises and crosses to* c.) No! You mustn't (*Leslie crosses to Charlie in a squat.*)

SARAH. (*Rises.*) Leslie says we must. (*As a comfort.*)

NANCY. No!

LESLIE. (*Puts his paw out.*) This *is* how we do it, isn't it?

SARAH. (*Watching; tentative.*) Such a wonderful thing to want to do. (*Charlie takes Leslie's paw. They shake hands.*)

LESLIE. (*Tight; formal.*) Thank you very much.

NANCY. No!

CHARLIE. You're welcome.

NANCY. NO!

LESLIE. (*Sighs.*) Well. (*Leslie and Sarah start moving up to the* u. *dune to exit. Leslie via* l. *ridge to* u. l. *pinnacle—Sarah via steps* r. *to top ridge* u. r. c.)

NANCY. (*In place.*) Please? (*Nancy moves to follow them onto first step.*)

SARAH. It's all right; it's all right.

NANCY. You'll have to come back . . . sooner or later. You don't have any choice. Don't you know that? You'll have to come back up.

LESLIE. (*Sad smile.*) *Do* we?

NANCY. Yes!

LESLIE. *Do* we have to?

NANCY. Yes!

LESLIE. Do we *have* to?

NANCY. (*Timid.*) We could *help* you. Please?

LESLIE. (*Anger and doubt.*) How!

CHARLIE. (*Sad, shy.*) Take you by the hand. (*Nancy goes to Charlie—kneels behind him.*) You've got to *do* it—sooner or later.

NANCY. (*Shy.*) We *could* help you. (*Leslie pauses; descends a step down from* u. l. *pinnacle to* u. l. *rock step; crouches; gives Sarah a look; stares at Charlie and Nancy.*)

LESLIE. (*Straight.*) All right. Begin.

CURTAIN

COSTUME LIST

NANCY
  Blue pants with white stitches
  Yellow shirt blouse
  Blue yarn hair ribbon for pony tail
  Gold bracelet
  No shoes or stockings
CHARLIE
  Faded blue jeans
  Pattern blue shirt
  Belt
  Chukka boots
  No socks
SARAH and LESLIE
  Lizard costumes made of milliskin stretch material with painted lizard
    markings.
  Hoods for the head with the face area visible. The face was created with
    make-up. Black eye lids with white circle around each eye and a black
    line outside white circle. Green avocado and mustard color with scale-
    like lines.

PROPERTY LIST

Act I

  Blanket spread on mark
  Pillow left side of blanket
On Blanket:
  Picnic hamper with lid closed but not latched
  Spread out
    2 paper napkins
    2 plates
    2 forks
    2 knives
    2 paper cups
    Bottle of Riesling wine (empty)
    Liver paste wrapped in foil
    Brie wrapped in foil
    Container wrapped in foil
    Butter dish (covered)
On r. Ridge
  Small twig-like stick

On U. R. RIDGE
    Artist's paint box open
    Small canvas
    Open paint tin box with 2 brushes
    Plastic container of water with lid (open)
    Paint cloth in paint box & other supplies
U. L. PINNACLE
    Large stick

ACT II

STRIKE:
    Small stick (near hamper)
    Spread out blanket again
    Put picnic hamper & pillow more up stage & tuck pillow so it will not
      move too readily.

NOTE: Since the ground plan consists of many levels, these terms were used
        to identify areas:
TOP RIDGE:
    The Upstage Center dune
RIGHT DUNE:
    The Right stage high area
RIGHT RIDGE:
    Ridge above Right path
STEPS:
    U. R. C. steps to paint box
CENTER ROCK:
    Rock Center below Upstage Center dune
LEFT RIDGE:
    Left raised rock formation leading up to the Left side of the Upstage Center
      dune
LEFT ROCK:
    Rock Left of Left ridge
UP LEFT PINNACLE:
    The Left end of the Upstage Center dune

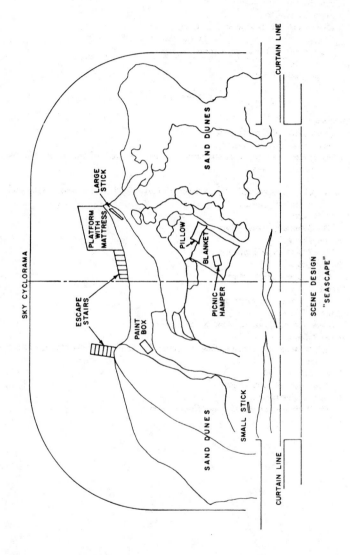

SKY CYCLORAMA

SAND DUNES

LARGE STICK

PLATFORM WITH MATTRESS

ESCAPE STAIRS

PILLOW

BLANKET

PAINT BOX

PICNIC HAMPER

SMALL STICK

SAND DUNES

CURTAIN LINE

CURTAIN LINE

SCENE DESIGN
"SEASCAPE"

59

NEW PLAYS

★ **MONTHS ON END by Craig Pospisil.** In comic scenes, one for each month of the year, we follow the intertwined worlds of a circle of friends and family whose lives are poised between happiness and heartbreak. "...a triumph...these twelve vignettes all form crucial pieces in the eternal puzzle known as human relationships, an area in which the playwright displays an assured knowledge that spans deep sorrow to unbounded happiness." –*Ann Arbor News.* "...rings with emotional truth, humor...[an] endearing contemplation on love...entertaining and satisfying." –*Oakland Press.* [5M, 5W] ISBN: 0-8222-1892-5

★ **GOOD THING by Jessica Goldberg.** Brings us into the households of John and Nancy Roy, forty-something high-school guidance counselors whose marriage has been increasingly on the rocks and Dean and Mary, recent graduates struggling to make their way in life. "...a blend of gritty social drama, poetic humor and unsubtle existential contemplation..." –*Variety.* [3M, 3W] ISBN: 0-8222-1869-0

★ **THE DEAD EYE BOY by Angus MacLachlan.** Having fallen in love at their Narcotics Anonymous meeting, Billy and Shirley-Diane are striving to overcome the past together. But their relationship is complicated by the presence of Sorin, Shirley-Diane's fourteen-year-old son, a damaged reminder of her dark past. "...a grim, insightful portrait of an unmoored family..." –*NY Times.* "MacLachlan's play isn't for the squeamish, but then, tragic stories delivered at such an unrelenting fever pitch rarely are." –*Variety.* [1M, 1W, 1 boy] ISBN: 0-8222-1844-5

★ **[SIC] by Melissa James Gibson.** In adjacent apartments three young, ambitious neighbors come together to discuss, flirt, argue, share their dreams and plan their futures with unequal degrees of deep hopefulness and abject despair. "A work...concerned with the sound and power of language..." –*NY Times.* "...a wonderfully original take on urban friendship and the comedy of manners—a *Design for Living* for our times..." –*NY Observer.* [3M, 2W] ISBN: 0-8222-1872-0

★ **LOOKING FOR NORMAL by Jane Anderson.** Roy and Irma's twenty-five-year marriage is thrown into turmoil when Roy confesses that he is actually a woman trapped in a man's body, forcing the couple to wrestle with the meaning of their marriage and the delicate dynamics of family. "Jane Anderson's bittersweet transgender domestic comedy-drama ...is thoughtful and touching and full of wit and wisdom. A real audience pleaser." –*Hollywood Reporter.* [5M, 4W] ISBN: 0-8222-1857-7

★ **ENDPAPERS by Thomas McCormack.** The regal Joshua Maynard, the old and ailing head of a mid-sized, family-owned book-publishing house in New York City, must name a successor. One faction in the house backs a smart, "pragmatic" manager, the other faction a smart, "sensitive" editor and both factions fear what the other's man could do to this house— and to them. "If Kaufman and Hart had undertaken a comedy about the publishing business, they might have written *Endpapers*...a breathlessly fast, funny, and thoughtful comedy ...keeps you amused, guessing, and often surprised...profound in its empathy for the paradoxes of human nature." –*NY Magazine.* [7M, 4W] ISBN: 0-8222-1908-5

★ **THE PAVILION by Craig Wright.** By turns poetic and comic, romantic and philosophical, this play asks old lovers to face the consequences of difficult choices made long ago. "The script's greatest strength lies in the genuineness of its feeling." –*Houston Chronicle.* "Wright's perceptive, gently witty writing makes this familiar situation fresh and thoroughly involving." –*Philadelphia Inquirer.* [2M, 1W (flexible casting)] ISBN: 0-8222-1898-4

DRAMATISTS PLAY SERVICE, INC.
440 Park Avenue South, New York, NY 10016 212-683-8960 Fax 212-213-1539
postmaster@dramatists.com www.dramatists.com

NEW PLAYS

★ **BE AGGRESSIVE by Annie Weisman.** Vista Del Sol is paradise, sandy beaches, avocado-lined streets. But for seventeen-year-old cheerleader Laura, everything changes when her mother is killed in a car crash, and she embarks on a journey to the Spirit Institute of the South where she can learn "cheer" with Bible belt intensity. "...filled with lingual gymnastics...stylized rapid-fire dialogue..." *–Variety.* "...a new, exciting, and unique voice in the American theatre..." *–BackStage West.* [1M, 4W, extras] ISBN: 0-8222-1894-1

★ **FOUR by Christopher Shinn.** Four people struggle desperately to connect in this quiet, sophisticated, moving drama. "...smart, broken-hearted...Mr. Shinn has a precocious and forgiving sense of how power shifts in the game of sexual pursuit...He promises to be a playwright to reckon with..." *–NY Times.* "A voice emerges from an American place. It's got humor, sadness and a fresh and touching rhythm that tell of the loneliness and secrets of life...[a] poetic, haunting play." *–NY Post.* [3M, 1W] ISBN: 0-8222-1850-X

★ **WONDER OF THE WORLD by David Lindsay-Abaire.** A madcap picaresque involving Niagara Falls, a lonely tour-boat captain, a pair of bickering private detectives and a husband's dirty little secret. "Exceedingly whimsical and playfully wicked. Winning and genial. A top-drawer production." *–NY Times.* "Full frontal lunacy is on display. A most assuredly fresh and hilarious tragicomedy of marital discord run amok...absolutely hysterical..." *–Variety.* [3M, 4W (doubling)] ISBN: 0-8222-1863-1

★ **QED by Peter Parnell.** Nobel Prize-winning physicist and all-around genius Richard Feynman holds forth with captivating wit and wisdom in this fascinating biographical play that originally starred Alan Alda. "QED is a seductive mix of science, human affections, moral courage, and comic eccentricity. It reflects on, among other things, death, the absence of God, travel to an unexplored country, the pleasures of drumming, and the need to know and understand." *–NY Magazine.* "Its rhythms correspond to the way that people—even geniuses—approach and avoid highly emotional issues, and it portrays Feynman with affection and awe." *–The New Yorker.* [1M, 1W] ISBN: 0-8222-1924-7

★ **UNWRAP YOUR CANDY by Doug Wright.** Alternately chilling and hilarious, this deliciously macabre collection of four bedtime tales for adults is guaranteed to keep you awake for nights on end. "Engaging and intellectually satisfying...a treat to watch." *–NY Times.* "Fiendishly clever. Mordantly funny and chilling. Doug Wright teases, freezes and zaps us." *–Village Voice.* "Four bite-size plays that bite back." *–Variety.* [flexible casting] ISBN: 0-8222-1871-2

★ **FURTHER THAN THE FURTHEST THING by Zinnie Harris.** On a remote island in the middle of the Atlantic secrets are buried. When the outside world comes calling, the islanders find their world blown apart from the inside as well as beyond. "Harris winningly produces an intimate and poetic, as well as political, family saga." *–Independent (London).* "Harris' enthralling adventure of a play marks a departure from stale, well-furrowed theatrical terrain." *–Evening Standard (London).* [3M, 2W] ISBN: 0-8222-1874-7

★ **THE DESIGNATED MOURNER by Wallace Shawn.** The story of three people living in a country where what sort of books people like to read and how they choose to amuse themselves becomes both firmly personal and unexpectedly entangled with questions of survival. "This is a playwright who does not just tell you what it is like to be arrested at night by goons or to fall morally apart and become an aimless yet weirdly contented ghost yourself. He has the originality to make you feel it." *–Times (London).* "A fascinating play with beautiful passages of writing..." *–Variety.* [2M, 1W] ISBN: 0-8222-1848-8

DRAMATISTS PLAY SERVICE, INC.
440 Park Avenue South, New York, NY 10016 212-683-8960 Fax 212-213-1539
postmaster@dramatists.com www.dramatists.com

NEW PLAYS

★ **SHEL'S SHORTS by Shel Silverstein.** Lauded poet, songwriter and author of children's books, the incomparable Shel Silverstein's short plays are deeply infused with the same wicked sense of humor that made him famous. "…[a] childlike honesty and twisted sense of humor." *—Boston Herald.* "…terse dialogue and an absurdity laced with a tang of dread give [*Shel's Shorts*] more than a trace of Samuel Beckett's comic existentialism." *—Boston Phoenix.* [flexible casting] ISBN: 0-8222-1897-6

★ **AN ADULT EVENING OF SHEL SILVERSTEIN by Shel Silverstein.** Welcome to the darkly comic world of Shel Silverstein, a world where nothing is as it seems and where the most innocent conversation can turn menacing in an instant. These ten imaginative plays vary widely in content, but the style is unmistakable. "…[*An Adult Evening*] shows off Silverstein's virtuosic gift for wordplay…[and] sends the audience out…with a clear appreciation of human nature as perverse and laughable." *—NY Times.* [flexible casting] ISBN: 0-8222-1873-9

★ **WHERE'S MY MONEY? by John Patrick Shanley.** A caustic and sardonic vivisection of the institution of marriage, laced with the author's inimitable razor-sharp wit. "…Shanley's gift for acid-laced one-liners and emotionally tumescent exchanges is certainly potent…" *—Variety.* "…lively, smart, occasionally scary and rich in reverse wisdom." *—NY Times.* [3M, 3W] ISBN: 0-8222-1865-8

★ **A FEW STOUT INDIVIDUALS by John Guare.** A wonderfully screwy comedy-drama that figures Ulysses S. Grant in the throes of writing his memoirs, surrounded by a cast of fantastical characters, including the Emperor and Empress of Japan, the opera star Adelina Patti and Mark Twain. "Guare's smarts, passion and creativity skyrocket to awesome heights…" *—Star Ledger.* "…precisely the kind of good new play that you might call an everyday miracle…every minute of it is fresh and newly alive…" *—Village Voice.* [10M, 3W] ISBN: 0-8222-1907-7

★ **BREATH, BOOM by Kia Corthron.** A look at fourteen years in the life of Prix, a Bronx native, from her ruthless girl-gang leadership at sixteen through her coming to maturity at thirty. "…vivid world, believable and eye-opening, a place worthy of a dramatic visit, where no one would want to live but many have to." *—NY Times.* "…rich with humor, terse vernacular strength and gritty detail…" *—Variety.* [1M, 9W] ISBN: 0-8222-1849-6

★ **THE LATE HENRY MOSS by Sam Shepard.** Two antagonistic brothers, Ray and Earl, are brought together after their father, Henry Moss, is found dead in his seedy New Mexico home in this classic Shepard tale. "…His singular gift has been for building mysteries out of the ordinary ingredients of American family life…" *—NY Times.* "…rich moments …Shepard finds gold." *—LA Times.* [7M, 1W] ISBN: 0-8222-1858-5

★ **THE CARPETBAGGER'S CHILDREN by Horton Foote.** One family's history spanning from the Civil War to WWII is recounted by three sisters in evocative, intertwining monologues. "…bittersweet music—[a] rhapsody of ambivalence…in its modest, garrulous way…theatrically daring." *—The New Yorker.* [3W] ISBN: 0-8222-1843-7

★ **THE NINA VARIATIONS by Steven Dietz.** In this funny, fierce and heartbreaking homage to *The Seagull*, Dietz puts Chekhov's star-crossed lovers in a room and doesn't let them out. "A perfect little jewel of a play…" *—Shepherdstown Chronicle.* "…a delightful revelation of a writer at play; and also an odd, haunting, moving theater piece of lingering beauty." *—Eastside Journal (Seattle).* [1M, 1W (flexible casting)] ISBN: 0-8222-1891-7

DRAMATISTS PLAY SERVICE, INC.
440 Park Avenue South, New York, NY 10016 212-683-8960 Fax 212-213-1539
postmaster@dramatists.com www.dramatists.com